READING IS ONLY THE TIGER'S TAIL

READING
is ONLY *the* TIGER'S TAIL

A LANGUAGE ARTS PROGRAM

Robert A. McCracken
Marlene J. McCracken

Peguis Publishers Limited   *520 Hargrave Street*   *Winnipeg Canada R3A 0X8*

Canadian Cataloguing in Publication Data

McCracken, Robert A., 1926-

   Reading is only the tiger's tail

   Previously published: Kimberley, B.C.: Classroom
Publications, ©1985.
   Bibliography: p.
   Includes index.
   ISBN 0-920541-13-5

1. Language arts (Primary) 2. English language —
Study and teaching (Primary) 3. Reading (Primary)
I. McCracken, Marlene J., 1932-   II. Title.

LB1528.M33 1986   372.6'044   C86-098083-9

Printing History
First printed, 1972, San Rafael, California
Seven printings to 1980
Eighth printing, 1985, Kimberley, B.C.
This edition, Revised, 1987.
Reprinted, March, 1987.
Reprinted, December, 1988.

Printed in Canada

CONTENTS

INTRODUCTION TO THIS EDITION

When we first wrote this book in 1970-71 we did not expect to be creating a second edition fifteen years later. We are pleased to have the chance to do so. RIOTT, today, is part of the swell of "Whole Language," a term or movement that did not exist in 1972. We hope that whole language may be understood so that it is more than an educational fad cresting and crashing onto a barren shore to be absorbed back into the salty waters. Education has seemed to be a series of disappearing swells. Phonics comes and goes; various programmed learning series have done the same; *Ita* is no longer a recognized acronym; SRA boxes are still visible, mostly in closets. Only the ubiquitous basal reader survives with its new covers and packaging.

Whole language is not a program, although some whole language "series" are appearing. It is a way of teaching that defies packaging. Whole language is psychologically and philosophically different than the current methods and those popularly used since 1950. Whole language asserts that:

1. Meaning and concepts are central to language learning. Form evolves from using language. Thus, speech evolved as man learned to express ideas that were stored in his brain. Writing evolved to record thoughts or facts. Meanings were in the brain before there was any need for language.

2. Language skills are a result of trying to make sense of speech or print. We never just *learn to read;* we *read to learn,* which results in learning to read.

3. There is no skill sequence. A child who is beginning to learn to speak or read or write makes gross attempts that are hardly recognizable as the final skill. A child scribbles. A child holds a book and babbles. Beginning skills evolve from gross attempts in erratic and idiosyncratic ways. (It may be that the basic skills that are the heart and soul of accountability tests are single skills measured in a multiplicity of ways.)

4. Language learning is a social, non-competitive process in which pupils share and communicate. Language skills are learned through practice. Children learn to speak readily because most parents and all peers respond to the messages ignoring the "errors" or lack of skill. Children practice freely without penalty for error. Most school programs demand correctness, and penalize error so there is little practice at beginning stages. Programs which attempt to eliminate or minimize error, minimize or eliminate learning. As a corollary, remedial programs designed to eliminate error, must fail. Tests, answer keys, and grades vitiate the process and prevent all children from optimum learning.

5. The minimum text from which reading can begin is the whole poem, song, story, or experience. All of the pieces must be available if the child is to understand any piece and how it functions. We cannot and should not attempt to determine what a child learns first; we must be sure that all the pieces are present and that the child works with the text to solve some of the mystery. Of course, we teach ways of working with text so that children share insights and learn efficiently, and we observe what has been learned and build instruction upon that.

6. Whole language is developmental. Skills mature, grow, and develop forever. No skill is ever mastered. Practice is always needed to maintain and develop skill.

7. There is no disintegration of language into components of listening, reading, writing, penmanship, spelling,

phonics, and speaking with separate instructional times. The language skills are integrated by focusing upon the content being learned and practising the skills that most naturally evolve.

8. Apprehension and expectation are two mutual conditions that enable the brain to direct the eye (or the ear when learning to speak) so that the text form can be understood and learned. Apprehension develops through repeated exposures to the same text. This is the magic of the favorite bed time story. This is why reading to children, and why reading a favorite story fifty or more times is basic readiness for solving text.

9. Children are capable of literacy if they are not so badly mistaught that they become confused and frustrated about how the form works. The human brain is built to learn language, and it does so if the whole of language is available.

Most of these beliefs were present in the original RIOTT although they were not formally stated.

In the original book, RIOTT is referred to frequently as a program. We considered removing the word "program" but have decided against it. However, we maintain that whole language is not a "program," nor is RIOTT a program. It is a way of working with children; it is a belief in children and childhood; it is belief in children's literature; it is a belief in teachers and their abilities to work with children in productive ways.

Whole language may be pictured as one end of a continuum with basal readers and phonics at the other. See below.

WHOLE LANGUAGE

THE STORY ⎫
   POEM ⎬ ... paragraph ... sentence ... phrase
   SONG ⎭ ... word ... syllable ... letter

BASAL READERS
PHONICS SYSTEMS

Instruction in whole language begins with the whole story; at some point the children begin to work with some of the pieces, but only with pieces that they know fit into a recognized puzzle.

For years people have argued and done research to determine if phonics or basal readers best teach a child to read. Phonics methods all focus on either the individual letters or syllables and their sounds. Basals focus on the word and use varying degrees of phonics. The goal of both phonics and basal readers is to learn sight words so that words may be "read" to get meaning. It is not surprising that there is no consistent result in the thousands of studies comparing phonics versus basal reading. They are both the same method.

Whole language methodology is different. Whole stories are read and re-read and memorized and practiced so that children read whole stories before they recognize the words or all the words. Through reading and writing they learn to recognize the words. Word recognition is the result of having learned to read and write, not the precursor.

Writing begins with something to say. The whole idea is in the child's head. The child now learns about the pieces — the words or letters — as he learns to write. Spelling is an outgrowth of learning to write, not a prerequisite. Penmanship is an outgrowth of learning to write, not a prerequisite. The acquisition of skills is the result of whole language instruction. However, the goal is the learning of content and concepts, and learning to communicate thoughts to others.

We have changed some parts of RIOTT in this edition. We have some different examples of children's work that seem more appropriate. We have added to the achievement section; we have eliminated some of the section on open education, one of the fads that crashed on barren shores. We have not tried to update with additional methods. This we have done in our books *Reading, Writing and Language* and *Stories, Songs and Poetry To Teach Reading and Writing.*

Robert and Marlene McCracken,
Surrey, B.C.
November, 1986.

ACKNOWLEDGMENTS

This book began as long as fifty years ago with Mrs. Winnefred Sheppard in a one-teacher school in rural British Columbia, and was transmitted to her daughter, Marlene Sheppard McCracken. But we know that the ideas in this book started even before that. We have taught for twenty or more years and have lost track of where the ideas emerged. They have converged in this book as ours, but we know that they have come from the thousands of pupils who have served as our teachers, the hundreds of teachers who have been our colleagues, our university professors who taught us, and most recently from the teachers who have worked with us in trying the RIOTT program.

We single out some people for special thanks, with trepidation lest we leave someone out. For three years or more we have been borrowing, begging, and collecting the samples of children's work that appear in this book. We collected many items before we even knew that there would be a book. Children, rightly so, are proud of their work and are reluctant to part with it, since they reread and reuse their writings. So first, we thank the children, who remain mostly anonymous, for the work they shared with us.

We thank the teachers and the personnel of the following school districts who have worked with us during the past few years: Richmond and Sardis (British Columbia, Canada); Great Falls (Montana); Burlington (Vermont); Ferndale, Arlington, Anacortes, Blaine, Sedro-Woolley, Burlington, Custer, Cusick, Port Angeles, and Bainbridge Island (Washington); Modesto and Riverside (California); and Zuni (New Mexico).

We want especially to thank the following teachers: Mrs. Peg Billings, Mrs. Madelyn Blackstone, Mrs. Marilyn Brandenburg, Mrs. June Chiba, Mrs. Florence Cragerud, Mrs. Jennifer Drake, Mrs. Georgia Foster, Mr. John Groom, Mrs. Roberta Hay, Mrs. Virginia Hayhurst, Mrs. Maryanne Larsen, Mrs. Sharon Lipscomb, Mrs. Alberta Macht, Mrs. Joanne Millican, and Mrs. Yvonne Walberg.

We want to acknowledge the friendship and inspiration over a period of many years of Dr. William D. Sheldon of Syracuse University; the thinking of Dr. Lyman C. Hunt, Jr., of the University of Vermont, who shared his ideas over a period of twenty years; and the insightful questioning of Mr. Wilf Graham, Superintendent, and Mr. Jack Lowe, Director of Elementary Instruction, of the Richmond Schools in British Columbia, who supported the use of the RIOTT program in the Richmond Schools as it developed.

Robert and Marlene McCracken,
Surrey, B.C., 1972.

PREFACE TO THE FIRST EDITION

There is no such thing as an effective reading program that does not embrace *all* of the language arts--and their interrelationships.

Traditionally, the skill acquisition sequence of the language arts has been: listening, speaking, reading, and writing. *Decoding has preceded encoding.*

But is the traditional sequence of the language arts the sequence that provides the greatest motivation and the greatest learning? The authors of this book think not, and they have backed up their premises with specific teaching suggestions based upon empirical evidence--with exciting examples of what children have done under the *Reading is only the Tiger's Tail* (RIOTT) program.

But what *is* this program? The only way to answer this question is to read all of this teacher's guide. Some teachers may wish to skim through the book first and then read it more carefully. Some teachers may decide to read Chapter Six before reading Chapter One, which is fine. The important thing is for the teacher to study *all* of this guide before embarking on the RIOTT program.

Ideally, the program should begin when the school year begins, but it can begin any time--whenever the teacher is ready. Experience has proved that the children are always ready--ready to learn because of the stimulation and motivation that this program provides.

ABOUT THE ILLUSTRATIONS

Children's art and early writings are big, uninhibited and color-ful, so it has seemed a little like squeezing a butterfly into a medi-cine capsule to fit them into the book. The works still impart a sense of energetic learning, but we wish they could have been reproduced in all their original exuberance! To all the young ar-tists and writers, our apologies.
The Publisher

Chapter I

CHILDREN'S BOOKS *and the* TEACHING *of* READING

In teaching reading, early success is vital. It is vital because children *want* to read.

1. Why children want to read.

Children read for entertainment, but other entertainments compete so well that reading for entertainment is not enough to compel children to read. Children demand more than entertainment. They want more than the ephemerality of television. They want to grow; they want to think; they want to speculate; they want to imagine; they want to learn. They want to feel secure--to feel that they are a part of humanity.

Children respond to inner pacings that cannot be met by moving stimuli. They want to look at a flower, to reflect about the stars, to feel the wind, to empathize with others. They want time to think; they want to shop in the world of ideas without pressure to buy. With books children can do this. They can listen to the voices of others, and they can respond in a hundred ways, knowing that each writer is mute and cannot censure their responses.

In reading, children have the freedom to live vicariously and to learn without penalty or time limit. They can reread and reread and reread as they think and think and feel and learn.

2. Why man writes.

Man writes to comment about human life, to preserve what he feels is fine--to enable the reader, now and many years hence, to improve the quality of human life. Man attempts to preserve the eternal, to leave a heritage of beauty and ideas. He hopes his observations are sage, his insights true, and that the reader may use his perceptions as mosaic tiles in developing patterns for understanding humanity.

To the degree that an author is successful, his works are read and reread by succeeding generations. As language changes, the message may be obscured; an older, more sophisticated reader may be needed. A children's literary classic sometimes is preserved by adults because children no longer have the requisite background to understand the story. Thus *Tom Sawyer* has moved from the general eight-to-twelve-year-old category to at least the twelve-to-sixteen-year-old category, and it seems most appreciated in college. The same can be said of Lewis Carroll's *Alice in Wonderland*, a children's book when written--now an adult classic.

3. What literature is.

Perhaps the outstanding characteristic of literature compared to an ordinary story is that literature is not tarnished by repetition; it gains a patina from use. An increasing depth of understanding comes with each rereading or retelling. Beauty of today, a timely comment, or an observation of the moment may lose poignancy. The modern, the sparkling, the hygienic may not age well and may be discarded without remorse. Literature of the moment is hard to judge; true literature is rediscovered and preserves itself.

Children have a natural ability to select literature and to force preservation. *Peter Rabbit* maintains its hold despite what might seem to be archaic language. What child of today has had camomile tea? No matter--almost every child has gone to bed ailing, to be soothed by his own mother's special concoction. The love involved is eternal; the archaic camomile understood and learned.

'Twas the Night Before Christmas will always be doggerel, but its message will continue to overcome its form. Children will have their wish; Donder and Blitzen will run the wintry

skies with or without Rudolph and his red nose. Rudolph's challenge, at best, is to join, not to displace.

The Little Engine That Could will still run, puffing along, trying, even though railroads are largely displaced by cars and trucks, to say nothing of airplanes. The Little Engine succeeds not because children are romantics who must be fed nectar, but because children are ordinarily willing to try the impossible.

Robert McCloskey's ducklings have charmed children for twenty-odd years and will probably charm them for many more. Birth is eternal, as are night and day, and this is affirmed in *Make Way for Ducklings.* Pierre will learn to care again and again as Maurice Sendak's hero is eaten by the lion and returned to life with each reading. The unreal is believable because the message is life itself.

E. B. White's spider, Charlotte, and pig, Wilbur, express the same importance of caring. With caring for another, with having known love, even a pig can face the real world. It is perhaps simplistic, but love and nurturing are eternal qualities that children understand. Children respond to these with an instant empathy. As literature portrays the eternal, it lives through succeeding generations.

4. **What reading is.**

Reading is the interpretation of alphabetic symbols and the use or application of the ideas interpreted. Sometimes the use is an overt action; sometimes it is only thought. Frank Jennings well defined reading as follows:

> *What is reading? Where does it start? How can it be done well? With these questions you can make a fortune, wreck a school system or get elected to the board of education. Most people who try to think about reading at all conjure up these little black wriggles on a page and then mutter something about "meaning." If this is all it is, very few of us would ever learn anything. For reading is older than printing or writing or even language itself. Reading begins with wonder at the world about us. It starts with the recognition of repeated events like thunder,*

lightning and rain. It starts with the seasons and the growth of things. It starts with an ache that vanished with food or water. It occurs when time is discovered. Reading begins with the management of signs of things. It begins when the mother, holding the child's hand says that a day is "beautiful" or "cold" or that the wind is "soft." Reading is "signs and portents," the flight of birds, the changing moon, the "changeless" sun and the "fixed" stars that move through the night. Reading is the practical management of the world about us. It was this for the man at the cave's mouth. It is this for us at the desk, the bench, or control panel.

The special kind of reading that you are doing now is the culmination of all the other kinds of reading. You are dealing with the signs of the things represented. You are dealing with ideas and concepts that have no material matter or substance and yet are "real." But you cannot do this kind of reading if you have not become skilled in all the other kinds. Unless you know down from up, hot from cold, now from then, you could never learn to understand things that merely represent other things. You would have no language, as you now understand it, and you could not live in the open society of human beings. It is quite conceivable that a true non-reader can only survive in a mental hospital.[1]

Our goal in reading should be to develop adults who use books, who read silently, who read voluntarily, who are interested in books, and who apply what they have read to their lives. The present emphasis in reading instruction in the United States usually ignores the implications both of Jennings' definition and of our goal.

5.   Learning to read through children's books.

Reading is traditionally taught as a sequence of three steps: First, the child is taught to recognize printed words and to pronounce them when he sees them in print. Second, the child is taught to comprehend the material that he reads.

The second step generally is incorporated with the first, with the emphasis shifting to comprehension and study skills as the child masters word recognition. Third, the child is taught to be interested in books and to love the reading of books. This third step is rarely incorporated with the first two steps.

The present teaching of reading in the United States gives heavy emphasis to recognizing printed words, usually through phonics. The present teaching gives emphasis to developing comprehension, and largely ignores the third step--developing a love of books--as part of reading instruction.

As a result, we have developed a literate populace, but elementary and secondary students are overtaught and underpracticed as readers. They can read, but they don't, and they won't.

A natural way to teach reading is to reverse the order of these steps. First, a child learns to love books and stories; second, he learns that books are to be comprehended; third, he learns to recognize words. There is a deliberate emphasis upon *teaching* in the traditional sequence and upon *learning* in the *reversed* sequence.

The experience-language approach of RIOTT is consistent with our goal because it gives children's books primary attention, because it emphasizes sustained silent reading, because it emphasizes interpretation and application, and because it does not equate word-pronouncing ability with reading. RIOTT uses the language-experience approach that Roach Van Allen and others have picked up on and much of the key-word approach of Sylvia Ashton-Warner, but it puts the use of books and the reading of books in the primary position as the *first* step in learning to read.

6. **The lap technique.**

The lap technique, admittedly idealistic, helps to explain learning to read through books:

   A. The adults around an infant child read books, magazines, and newspapers. Since young children learn by imitation, this reading in front of children is mandatory.

   B. Mother and father put the child (aged six months to eighteen months for beginning) on their laps each day and hold a children's book. They talk about the pictures, they point, and eventually they read the text aloud. This continues for five or more years. This is an emotional conditioning to books; children associate books with love and warmth and parents.

C. The child between the ages of two and five begins taking these books. He sits alone with them for thirty minutes, an hour, an hour and a half. He opens the books, looks at them, and he talks out loud about them. He recites much of the text from memory. He is reading, if we use our definition of reading. He is interpreting symbols, he is reading silently, and he is making use of what he reads. He may not recognize any words, but he has learned that reading is fun, reading is enjoyable, and that reading is comprehending.

The authors know of a family where *The Man in the Manhole and The Fix-it Men*[2] has been read to each of the children:

> No one was on the street. It was a big empty quiet street with long morning shadows. It was was a silent sign on the empty street that said MEN AT WORK. But there were no men in sight, not even a cat. And everything was quiet and very still, not a sound, not even a smell. When suddenly . . .

> Up popped a man out of a manhole. He had a blue handkerchief around his neck, and a big hooked crowbar in one hand, and a big monkey wrench in the other.

> And he walked down the street until he came to the other manhole. He took his big crowbar and pried up the manhole lid. Then he leaned down the hole and shouted, "Ho, Joe!" The echo came back, *Ho, Joe*. Then from far away in the darkness a smaller voice hollered back, "Ho, Tonio!" *Ho, Tonio*.

There is a laundry chute in the house, and almost every piece of laundry flying down that chute is preceded by a call of "Ho, Joe!" If any member of the family is near one of the other openings of the laundry chute, a response flies back, "Ho, Tonio!" This may be disconcerting to strangers who hear the yell and the reply, followed by a swoosh as some heavy laundry rumbles down the chute. For the family, it is like the striking of the clock. For the child aged three or four, "Ho, Joe!" or "Ho, Tonio!" is applying reading to his life in a meaningful way.

A child who has had the lap technique comes to school ready to learn to recognize words, and in school he is taught word-recognition skills. The schools are excellent in teaching reading to those children who come to school ready. The schools cannot do an excellent job of teaching reading with those children who come to school less than ready if they begin by teaching reading as a word-recognition process.

Schools must provide the learnings of the lap technique for those children who never had a lap for reading. This takes years, not weeks or months, and it takes school time.

Even for those children who come to school having had the lap technique at home, the learnings of the lap technique should continue. All children need to be read to in the classroom.

7. **Reading to children in the classroom.**

Reading to children should be a part of every elementary teacher's program for children. Children should hear a good book, a chapter of a book, or a poem read orally to them every day.

Parents can be enlisted to help in this program. Parents can be scheduled to come to the classroom, sit in the reading corner, and be surrounded by, or sat upon (one at a time) by three to eight children as the parent reads orally. Children can sign up to be read to if a parent arrives, and the children can determine what book they want to hear read. Generally the reader should read something he loves when he reads to children, but many parents do not know children's books and feel very uncomfortable about choosing. Children's choosing of books to be read can solve this problem--and at the same time expand the parents' acquaintance with the wonderful world of children's books.

This use of parents has one important advantage over parents' tutoring or teaching: the parent can be very irregular in his attendance and yet not damage the RIOTT program.

8.   Sustained silent reading (SSR). *See also pages 151-153.*

Sustained silent reading (SSR) is an integral part of the program. It places emphasis upon children's comprehending and using books and, in the kindergarten particularly, it incorporates some of the lap technique into introducing books to children. The authors have observed many classes of children in kindergarten reading silently, sustaining themselves for long periods of time, even though the children recognized no words in print.

SSR is a concept formally labeled by Lyman C. Hunt, Jr., University of Vermont, who sees the goal in reading instruction as developing children who can sustain themselves without interruption in silent reading for periods of half an hour or more.

For example, a kindergarten teacher puts fifty to sixty children's picture books in a pile in the middle of the story-time rug. The children sit on the edge of the rug, surrounding the books. The teacher reaches in, takes one book from the pile, opens it, and reads a page or two orally. Then the teacher comments and puts the book back into the pile. The teacher takes another book, comments about its title and its author, reads a page or two, and puts the book back into the pile.

The teacher does this with books such as George Shannon's *Lizard's Song* and *Dance Away,* Aliki's *At Mary Bloom's,* Mirra Ginsburg's *The Chick and The Duckling,* and Robert and Marlene McCracken's *The Farmer and the Skunk* and *How Do You Say Hello to a Ghost?* She reads some of the books in 'Big Book' form tracking the print and having the children chime in on repeated parts. The teacher reads at least one entire book and puts it back into the pile. This introduction may take twenty to forty minutes, and this type of introduction is repeated many times.

Then the teacher says, "Today we are going to read silently, and we're going to sustain ourselves in silent reading.

Does anyone know what it means to sustain yourself in silent reading?" Probably no child knows, so the teacher explains: "This means that you're going to spend some time with one book, paying attention only to it, reading it and rereading it while looking at it very carefully. What do the pictures say? You know, you can read books without reading words."

The children are told that they will have one minute to choose a book, which they will read for a few minutes while sitting back on the edge of the rug. The children scramble into the middle. The book that the teacher has read all the way through is usually grabbed immediately, and the other books from which the teacher has read a page or two are grabbed next. The children crawl back to the edge of the rug. The teacher sets a minute timer (such as is used for cooking) and tells the children that they must read until the timer rings.

While the children read, the teacher opens a book, preferably an adult book, and reads it silently. If the teacher does not read, the children will think it's all right for them not to read. If the teacher answers questions, the children will think it's all right to talk. But if the teacher reads and ignores everything else, the children will read silently until the timer rings.

In kindergarten classes where teachers have used this approach in the teaching of reading, the children have read silently each day, sustaining themselves in a single book. Even more significantly, the children have demanded that they have a sustained silent reading period every day. And these children have quickly learned to sustain themselves in silent reading for fifteen to twenty minutes.

One kindergarten teacher reported success with two hyperactive boys who practically never sat down--not even at milk time nor lunch time. The teacher had felt sure that SSR would not work with these boys. But it did. The teacher began SSR in March (working up to fifteen minutes in the first two weeks) and continued through June. The two hyperactive boys sat down each day for fifteen minutes of sustained silent reading. These two boys still never sat down for milk time nor lunch time, nor anything else, but they did sit down for SSR. Books have a power--a power that is not predicated on the recognition of words.

There are also other ways in which SSR is different from traditional reading practice. In SSR there are no comprehension questions. There are no book reports. There is no record-keeping. There is only one requirement--the child must sustain himself in reading silently.

SSR is necessary at all grade levels so that every child gets the chance to practice reading every day. The authors have used SSR at all grade levels and have found little difficulty in establishing a minimum of thirty minutes of SSR.

There is difficulty, however, if the teacher does not believe that the pupils are reading and walks around or looks up to check. There is also difficulty if any record-keeping intrudes when SSR is initiated, although some record-keeping is accepted by pupils once they have the SSR habit. There is also difficulty when the teacher feels that a child cannot read a book if he does not recognize one of the words and when the teacher offers help in pronouncing words during SSR time.

A benefit of SSR that can hardly be overemphasized is its provision of an extensive supply of language models. Children learn through imitation--by copying models. Children who are exposed to a multitude of good books and read a great many such books will imitate the language of these books in their speaking and writing.

Many systems of teaching fail to provide superior models of language. They restrict children by vocabulary control that is based upon "known" words, used in an unnatural succession of short sentences. Children must have unrestricted language models to achieve language growth. Children must be exposed to figurative as well as literal language. They must be exposed to a wide range of standard English, especially if they come from an environment where standard English is seldom used.

A child will never learn the language without the freedom of opportunity. Good children's books can and do open the child's mind to the world of words, to the world of standard literacy. Good books do not demean a child's background nor his nonstandard, oral English. Instead, they provide a model that the child can emulate--a model that can be of great value to him in later years of his life.

Chapter II

THINKING *and* COMMUNICATION

Most children come to school with the ability to talk. They can talk about the things that they have experienced. They can communicate their experiences and their thoughts. But the language that the children use may not be standard English, and the teacher is faced with the task of leading children toward the goal of reading and writing standard English.

The instruction of each child must, of course, start where that child is. Beginning reading and writing must be taught through the child's own language. Then, gradually, with teaching and refinement, the child is led until he can read and write standard literary English. This may be accomplished in six months, six years, or more. Most pupils require years of instruction.

This instruction necessarily involves the skills of communication--the giving and getting of information and ideas or thoughts. To communicate, a pupil must think; he must have ideas to express or ideas that he wants to listen to. To reach the basic objectives of reading and writing, the teacher must teach so that children learn to think (even though "thinking" is not easy to define).

In considering communication, it is important to keep in mind that much of people's communication is nonverbal. Facial expressions, gestures, body movements, dress, art, music, and various symbols provide much nonverbal communication. In this RIOTT program, however, the major goal is the development of verbal communication--communication with words.

All verbal communication involves both sending and receiving. Sending is done through oral language (speaking) and writing. Receiving is done through listening and reading. This is represented in Figure 1.

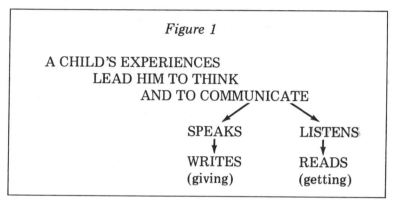

Figure 1

A CHILD'S EXPERIENCES
LEAD HIM TO THINK
AND TO COMMUNICATE

SPEAKS   LISTENS

WRITES   READS
(giving)   (getting)

When children begin school, they have already had numerous experiences from which they have conceived many thoughts, thoughts which they have shared with other children and adults. They have talked, listened, and talked some more. Children come to school communicating orally; they can speak and listen.

Their preschool experiences are the grist for thinking, the readiness for sharing ideas in class. In class children talk and listen to each other, and from their talking and listening they learn to write and then read, and then talk some more. All four areas are vital, so interrelated that they are equal in importance as facets of communication. The children are encouraged to use all of their senses to develop understanding of ideas and to learn to verbalize what they perceive through all of their senses.

Figure 1 should not be construed to mean that oral language experiences should be separated from, or subordinated to written language after written language has been introduced. Once children have begun to write, the oral and written aspects of language should be developed together, mutually reinforcing each other at every step of the way. All four components, listening, speaking, reading, and writing, are necessary for a successful language arts program.

But one of the biggest problems all teachers face is getting some children to listen. Some children are adept at listening, but other children seem unable to listen.

Listening is both a tuning in and a tuning out. In the cacophony of modern civilization, the sanity of children may depend as much on their ability to tune out as it does on their ability to tune in. The result of this tuning out is the apparently short attention span of the young child.

But do children really have such short attention span? Watch a child concentrating on a worm. Watch a child filling and refilling a hole in the sand with water. Watch a child staring at a television set--or even a picture book. Obviously children can pay attention to something for a very long period--if they are interested. Thus the teacher's problem is to find out what will both *interest* and *educate*. The teacher must get the children's attention and hold it.

One major method of getting children's attention is to get them to *listen*. Like adults, children will listen if they are enjoying something, and *they will listen if they are learning*. People of all ages tend to listen most attentively when they are trying to learn or discover something.

But listening is not simply hearing. It is much more. A normal child can hear sounds; he must be taught to listen to *thoughts*--to listen with a purpose--to develop listening skills.

All of the listening skills are, of course, language skills, and all of the language skills are, to a great extent, thinking skills. Some of the most frequently stressed of these skills are the following:

> getting the main idea
> understanding words in context
> recalling details
> remembering the sequence of events
> recognizing cause and effect
> making inferences
> drawing conclusions
> predicting outcomes.

All of the above skills and a number of others are commonly called *reading skills*. To label them solely as reading skills limits our perception and our teaching. All of these skills are language-thinking skills that may be taught through oral language--through listening and speaking.

This listening and speaking provides readiness for reading and writing, but the major emphasis in the RIOTT program is upon *thinking* and *communicating*.

The beginning program has two strands. The first strand is the development of concepts and vocabulary, to which this chapter will be devoted. (The second strand is the development of an awareness of sounds, which is covered in Chapter Three.) Strands One and Two have been separated for explication. Yet in teaching, Strands One and Two are inseparable, and are developed simultaneously. The development of concepts and vocabulary is the raw material for the beginnings of reading and writing.

Most of the motivational work, most of the thinking to develop concepts and vocabulary, and most of the theme work is done by teaching the whole class as a group. Individual differences are not ignored. Provision for individual differences and individual skill teaching is through the handling of each child's individual responses. Total class involvement is essential to provide the necessary stimuli for discussions (and for the most efficient use of the teacher's time), even though classes may have difficulty in learning how to respond productively to total class participation.

Thinking and communicating are stimulated by having children talk to each other. The teacher leads one child as he talks to the class. The class listens. The child speaking comes to realize that his ideas are worthy of an audience; he learns that what he says is important to someone else.

The child has always wanted to communicate, but he has not always had an attentive audience. He has a need now to express himself clearly and coherently. The teacher can guide him in developing his skill in oral communication. Each child develops something of a sense of personal worth and, usually, a recognition of the worth of his classmates. (Children should not be forced to talk. Instead, they should be allowed to wait until their interest overcomes their shyness.)

One child talks to the whole class about himself. The teacher questions the child as needed to elicit information. Most beginning stories are brief. The child (George) talks about himself, the funniest thing that ever happened, the scariest thing, the most exciting thing, etc. For example:

George: "The scariest thing was a big dog chased me." (George is allowed to go on without aid, but in the beginning children often go no farther, in which case the teacher asks questions.)

Teacher: "How did this happen?"

George: "I was going home from school, and a big dog jumped out at me and barked and barked as I was walking by."

Teacher: "Where did this happen?"

George: "At the corner by Jones's Store."

Teacher: "What did you do?"

George: "I ran home and jumped in my father's car and slammed the door and locked it securely."

The teacher may elicit more, but this is enough. The teacher now questions the audience. The teacher asks three kinds of questions. She asks questions to:

1. develop thinking skills, recall, inference, drawing conclusions, etc.
2. elicit empathy and identification.
3. develop vocabulary.

First, the teacher wants to make the listeners think, to remember the story, and to discuss it:

Teacher: "What was the main idea of George's story?"

Pupil: "George was scared by a big dog."

Teacher: "When did this happen?"

Another pupil: "George was going home from school."

Teacher: "What did George do when the dog chased
him?" etc.

Next, the teacher wants to make the listeners go beyond
recall and sequence:

Teacher: "Why do you think the dog chased
George?"

Pupil: "The dog wanted to bite George."

Teacher: "Yes, that might be the reason. Can you
think of another reason the dog chased
George?"

Another
pupil: "The dog might have wanted to play."

Teacher: "Yes, that is another possibility. Can you
think of any other reasons the dog might
have chased George?"

Another
pupil: "The dog might have thought George was
a friend."

Another
pupil: "The dog might have thought he was the
newspaper boy. Our dog always chases the
newspaper boy."

The teacher elicits many answers to these questions and
moves on:

Teacher: "Do you think George will run home the
same way after this?"

Teacher: "What do you think might have happened
if George hadn't jumped into his father's
car?"

As the pupils respond to these questions, the teacher asks
"why?" or "why not?"

Next, the teacher wants to make the listeners identify
with George--to feel some of the feelings George felt:

Teacher: "How do you think George felt when he
was running?"

"How do you think George felt when he
slammed the car door?"

"How long do you think George stayed in
the car?"

"How long would you have stayed?"

As the children answer, the teacher uses their answers to direct further questions. No attempt is made to elicit a response from each child. No attempt is made to get the maximum number of responses. The objective is simply to extend thinking.

Finally, the teacher wants to make the children aware of the words George used and to extend their vocabulary. The teacher will pay particular attention to any unusual words that George used.

Teacher: "George said he locked the car door *securely*. What does *securely* mean? How else might you say the same thing?"

Pupils: "It was locked tight."
"The dog couldn't get it open."
"Quickly."
"So no one could get in unless George let them."

Teacher: "If you tie your shoelaces *securely*, how do you tie them?"

Pupils: "So they won't come loose."
"They will stay tied even if you run."

The teacher tries to correct inadequacies of initial responses without saying that something is right or wrong. The teacher works with shades of meaning and tries to relate an unknown word with similar known words.

Teacher: "Have you ever been frightened and run to your mother and hugged her and felt secure? How did you feel?"

Teacher: "How does a door sound when it is slammed? What other words could George have used to describe slamming the door?"

At this point, the teacher might write the words *shut, closed, banged, pulled,* etc., on the chalkboard and discuss shades of meaning by questioning the children.

Teacher: "We have said George could have slammed the door, closed the door, shut the door, pulled the door closed. Which of these would have made the most noise?"

Pupils: (Several answers.)

Teacher: "Which would have been the quietest?"

Pupils: (Several answers.)
Teacher: "Which of these would George do quick-
           ly? Why?"
Pupils: (Several answers.)
Teacher: "Which of these would George have done
           slowly? Why?"

After a few weeks, the pupils anticipate the types of questions they will be asked, and they become active listeners. The pupils then ask questions of the child who has spoken to them. The teacher intervenes only if the questions do not cover a wide range of thinking skills, or if the questions fail to cover some skill or point that the teacher wants to emphasize.

As a speaker, each child learns that he is important. His ideas are used by the whole class. As a listener, each child learns that he is expected to think about what is being said so that he can later ask questions to clarify or expand the story or information. As a result of this participation, each listener learns that he is important. A mutual respect is built as each child learns that he is an important, contributing member of the class.

DEVELOPING COMMUNICATION

To provide a meaningful foundation of communicating, the teacher develops many activities for thought, or themes around which thoughts can be shared--a common ground for thinking. Some ways to provide this common ground are the following:

1. The theme "Myself"
2. Abstract ideas
3. Creative art
4. Sensory areas
5. Seasonal units
6. Picture activities
7. Using books, nursery rhymes, poems, and stories

1. Ways to develop the theme "Myself"

My family   1. Names and relationships
           Have each child make an autobiography to
           share with the class and to become part of the
           class library. Each of the following may be
           used for one page:

a. This is me. I'm Jeff.
b. This is my mom.
c. She likes to _____.
d. This is my dad.
e. He likes to _____.
f. This is my sister.
g. She likes to _____.
h. I like to _____.
i. I don't like to _____.

(or the book may be made to suit the taste of each pupil by having him dictate his ideas to be written down by a teacher or aide.)

My friends

1. Concept of a friend
2. Studying names

Discuss what a friend is. "Do friends always have to be people?" etc.

Tell who one's best friends are. Teacher writes names on chalkboard and begins to discuss the similarities in speech and print. (*See Chapter Three.*) Class stories may be made. Books about friends may be read.

My toys

1. Names and description
2. Classification

Have children bring toys to school and name and describe the toys for classmates. Gradually build a toy corner. Use this for classification. Allow children to group toys in different ways, such as:

a. girls' toys and boys' toys
b. toys that "go" and toys that don't "go"
c. various sizes
d. toys with wheels and without
e. various shapes
f. various colors, etc.

Label toys and use these labels to reinforce the phonics instruction and to give the children some words to use in writing. (*See Chapter Three.*)

My pets

1. Names and description
2. Classification

Children can cut out magazine pictures resembling their pets or pets they would like to have. These may be classified in many ways. Charts may be made after classification:

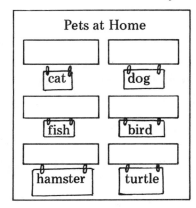

Labels may be affixed on by paper clips.

As children begin to learn beginning consonants, the labels may be removed by teacher, distributed, and replaced by children.

I

1. Knowledge of the word *I*
2. Parts of the body

Teach the word *I* so that the children can begin to write thoughts about themselves. Beginning encoding can be "I (and a picture)." Children read the word *I* and the message from a picture, e.g.,

could be read as "I like my wagon."
                "I have a wagon."
                "I can pull a wagon." etc.

Children become very interested in the various parts and functions of their bodies. This interest can become the basis of a beginning reading and writing program as described in Chapter Four. To stimulate this interest, various activities may be started.

a. Children may study themselves in a full mirror.

b. One child may lie on a large piece of paper placed on the floor, and another child may trace around him. When each child has an outline of himself, each may label, color, and post his outline.

c. Children may listen to each other's hearts with a stethoscope.

d. Children may watch their own mouths in a mirror while making sounds, so that they may become more aware of the physical aspects of speaking.

e. Children may feel each other's throats when they are speaking. Have them notice the vibrations of specific sounds, such as the sound of "hard" /g/.

Ways to develop subtheme "I."

My wishes Divide into two classifications--possible and impossible--to teach the concepts of true and make-believe. Follow up by reading stories about children in each of these classifications.

Things I'd like to have happen to me Discuss this in depth to help children begin to think about cause and effect.

Things I wouldn't like to have happen Ask "why?" and discuss in depth to promote more thinking about cause and effect.

What I'd like to do more than anything else	Ask "why?" and "how?" to teach the skill of predicting outcomes.
What I'd like to have more than anything else	"Why? What would you do with it? How would you use it? Describe it." Such questioning should promote vocabulary development.
TV shows I like to watch	Have the children discuss characters and plot.

The funniest thing that happened to me

The worst thing that happened to me

The nicest thing

The most exciting thing

The scariest thing, etc.

To teach vocabulary and understanding of words *funny, scary, nice,* etc., leading into a discussion of emotions.

The authors have discussed only a very few ideas or tangents from which communication grows in the theme **Myself**. Allowing the theme to grow according to the children's responses is imperative. In the preceding examples, the authors have illustrated how basic skills can be taught through a theme so that the teaching of basic skills is meaningful and relevant. The beginnings of reading and writing are embodied in the various activities as children are encouraged to record and share the thoughts developed in class discussion.

2. Abstract ideas.

The teacher leads the class in discussing feelings such as those of happiness, love, hate, friendship, kindness, jealousy, etc. Each child is led to discuss what each emotion is for him. The teacher questions to elicit full, thoughtful responses.

The following questions are only suggestions. The teacher must follow the class responses when expanding comprehension of abstract ideas.

Happiness   "How do you feel when you are happy?"
"Is it a nice feeling?"
"Do you feel happy when you make someone else happy? Why?"
"How can you make someone else happy?"
"Whom would you like to make happy? Why? How?"
"What is the thing that makes you the happiest? Why?"
"What words can describe how you feel when you are happy?"

The teacher must work hard and tenaciously when developing the vocabulary of abstract ideas. The goal is a multitude of responses. Initially, the number of responses may be limited, but the teacher must be both patient and persistent. Thinking takes practice, and it may be two or three months before the children respond freely and easily.

The discussion provides a good basis for making a class book. At the end of a discussion, each child may be given a sheet of paper and asked to draw or write what happiness means to him. Children at the very beginning stages who have no writing skills will, of course, need to draw.

The teacher moves from child to child, making sure that each child can verbalize what his picture represents. Suppose the child says, "Happiness is when your mother and father and sisters and aunts and uncles and brother all want to kiss you." The teacher writes this quickly at the top or bottom of the child's picture, comments to the child about his ideas, and moves on.

Suppose the next child says, "Happiness is my dog licking my face." The teacher writes this quickly and goes on to the next child. The teacher encourages the child to write any part of the sentence or any part of any word that the teacher thinks the child can write by himself.

The teacher works with the less able children first so that the more able children will be impatient enough to try writing. The teacher always writes exactly what the child dictates and prints clearly but hurriedly. The teacher should not set such a perfect model of writing that the child will be afraid to try to write as he learns encoding skills.

The teacher makes a cover for the book or has one of the children make a cover, which is titled *Happiness Is* . . . . The teacher collects all of the pictures and staples them together under the cover to make a class book.

The class can now read. Each child can read his own page at least, and is a potential teacher of his own page. Each pupil-teacher has a potential of perhaps thirty pupils. Each child is a potential reader of perhaps thirty pages.

Happiness elicited the following two responses from first-grade children in January 1970:

Misery evoked the following four expressions from second-grade children:

It was Misery when my first dog dide. I felt very very very sad. We had sort of a funrul. we bered the dog and then we had the funrul in Sisters room

Misery is being sick on ^{pamela} your Birthday and not having a Birthday Party!!! Misery is mising school!!!

I want to go to School

Misery Is whan my Big Siser Buose me I gut So mad I cold far her up.

Misesy Is geting a u on my Reading paper

Friends and *Friendship* inspired second-grade boys and girls to write the following. The first example is four pages long.

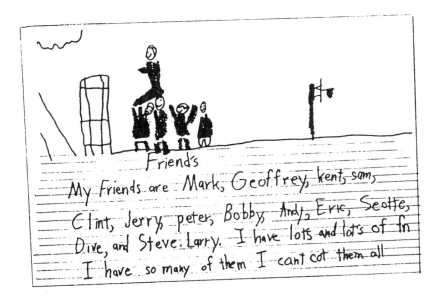

Friend's

My Friends are Mark, Geoffrey, kent, sam, Clint, Jerry, peter, Bobby, Andy, Eric, Seotte, Dive, and Steve. Larry. I have lots and lots of fn I have so many of them I cant cot them all

I ges all ciort them all. 1,2, 3, 4, 5, 6, 7, 8, 9, 10, 11, 12, 13, 14, 15, 16, 17, 18, 19, 20, 21, 22, 24, 25, 26, 27, 28, 29, 30, 31, 32, 33, 34, 36, 37, 38, 39, 40, 41, 42, 43, 44, 45, 46, 47, 50, 51, 52, 53, 54, 55, 56, 57, 58, 59, 60, 61, 64

63, 64, 65, 66, 67, 68, 67, 70, 71, 72, 73, 74, 75, 76, 77, 78, 79
80, 81, 82, 83, 84, 85, 86, 87, 88, 89, 90, 91, 92, 93, 94, 95, 96, 97,
98, 99, 100.1   I have too frinds. Boy did it take me a long
tihe to cxont all my frinds. Boy did it! We lke to share
together! helP together!   play together! and work together

I like to be nice to my friends. my friends like to be nice to me
I help them sometimes   I play with them   They play with
me They help me sime times. They share with me. I share
with them. I think I have nice friends I hop they think
the same way I did

I Friends! Peter March 22
My Friends are-1.Mark, 2.Terry, Andy,
4Geoffrey, 5Bobby, 6kent, 7sam, 8stere and 9Jer,
and10Eric. The way to make friends is
to work together Like if I wanted to

Theresa and Shelly are obviously good friends as they wrote about each other:

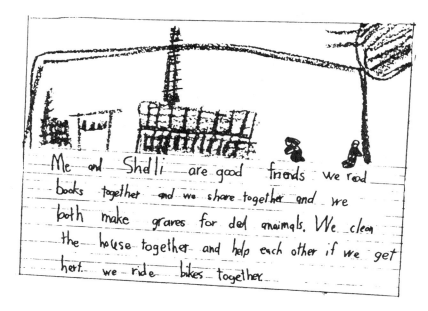

Me and Shelli are good friends we read books together and we share together and we both make graves for ded anoimals. We clean the house together and help each other if we get hert. we ride bikes together

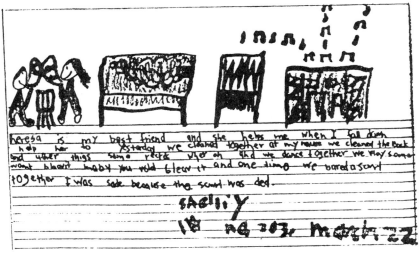

Theresa is my best friend and she helps me when I fall down. I help her to Ysterday we cleaned together at my house we cleaned the back and uther thigs sume redid vfo oh and we dance together we play some want blaovt maby you rold blew it and one time we bared a squrl together I was sade because the squrl was ded

SHelliY
18 na 303, march 22

3. Creative art.

Creativity, however it is defined, is an expression of an idea or ideas. Children need to understand that they are expressing an idea or ideas through their art. The media they choose for the telling (clay, construction paper, crayons, etc.), the shapes, and the content are all expressions that either help or hinder the telling of the thought. Children need help in exploring the values of different media, various colors, shapes, and content of expression. It is important that the teacher help the pupils in this quest.

It is the thought that counts when children do any type of creative art. The teacher must remember this, or art will easily degenerate into mere copying or reproduction. The teacher must help the children build ideas orally, challenge them to express their ideas in an art form, and then to use the ideas expressed through art to stimulate written expression.

Sometimes the art is the culminating expression. Too often, however, teachers challenge pupils to write and then to illustrate--and get disappointing results. For young children, the written form is the more difficult (as well as for many not-so-young children), so the art expression usually should precede the written work.

Color. Thoughts about color and an awareness of color can be introduced through "color" weeks. One week is devoted to red, the next to blue, the next to green, etc. During the red week, the teacher and the children bring articles and pictures for discussion and display in a *red corner*. The articles and pictures may be labeled and used by the teacher to reinforce the phonics that has been taught.

From the study of the *red corner,* the teacher builds an awareness of the various shades or hues of red--the reds that are natural, the reds that have been created by artists in their pictures, or the reds created in dyes--and the responses that reds can evoke within one's mind. ("Which red is the happiest?" "Which is the quietest?" etc.) The children should become aware of the feelings associated with red; the ways in which red may be used to express an idea; the red things that seem appropriately red; the things that might be appropriately red, but aren't; and the red things that might be better if they were a different color.

The teacher can have the children brainstorm about red. The responses will range from the mundane "red is an apple" to the poetic "red is the clouds at sunset" to the personal "red is my face when I strike out." Brainstorming for objects that are red can result in a noun-color book. Each child illustrates and completes a sentence such as "A _____ is red." Brainstorming for feelings and emotions can be stimulated by questions such as: "How does red make you feel?" "Is red noisy or quiet?" "How would you feel if this whole classroom were red and everything in it was red?" Such questioning can evoke poetic and highly imaginative responses to complete the frame "Red is _____."

Books such as Robert Bright's *I Like Red* will inspire thoughts about red and redness. Mary O'Neil's delightful *Hailstones and Halibut Bones* does this poetically. The color used in literally hundreds of excellent children's books can inspire thoughts even though the theme of the book is not directly about color.

The following thoughts were evoked in a first-grade class during an extensive study of color. (Note that these are in the children's own spelling. The objective here was not spelling instruction, but creative expression. Had the emphasis been upon spelling, much of the creative flow would have been stifled.)

> White is a see shell shining.
> White is the lituning coming down.
> White is milk and mshmeloe.
> Pink is a pig that has a krley tail.
> Pink is the wrms slithring thro the ground.
> Pink is a shie feeling.
> Purple is a broze when you fal of a pony.
> Purple is the sond of thundr.
> Purple is the night strting.
> Blue is shawdos on the snow.
> Blue is the oshin on a windy day.
> Green is the sun trikling throo the trees.
> Green is the smel of a deep frest.
> Green is cold water melin.

Yellow is supos to cheer you up.
Yellow is the sun dansing on the roks.
Yellow is the sun pransing on the leafs.
Yellow is a happy fase.
Orange is when you dont broosh your teeth.
Orange is the britest pees ov the ranebo.
Orange is the windose twingkling in the nite.

Shapes. Children need to be made aware of shapes--to observe and think. This awareness can be developed in many ways. The teacher may use squiggles, recognizable shapes such as squares, triangles, circles, cylinders, cubes, letters of the alphabet, or random scraps of construction paper. For example:

"Here is a squiggle."

"What could it be? Turn your paper every way you can. Think. Could you add something to this and make something from it? Is it alive? Is it real? Does it come from Mars?"

Allow the children to guess, reconsider, build on each other's ideas, and verbalize, until fifty or sixty ideas have been expressed. Then allow the children to complete the squiggle, color it, and name it.

"Here is a shape."

"What could it be? What could it be part of? Turn it. Could it be anything else?"

Again elicit *many* verbal responses. Children's work shows the results of thought development.

The following six examples were made by the children in a first-grade class. At this stage, some of the children created only a picture; some wrote only a simple caption; others wrote sentences. A total-group activity of this kind allows for individual expression at whatever level each child is capable--truly individualized learning.

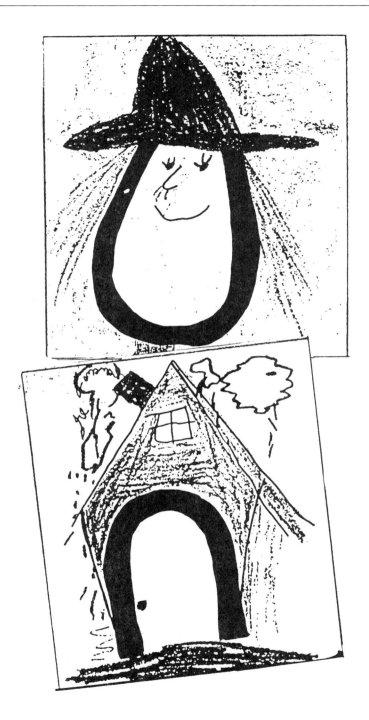

This is a hall what the rabbi ate his carit in It is a big wun

Ta nya

end of a horse this is a horse. the end of

These six were created by first-grade and second-grade children. For one child, the drawn expression was complete. He chose not to write, even though encouraged to and even though he knew how to write. His teacher wisely did not insist upon his writing.

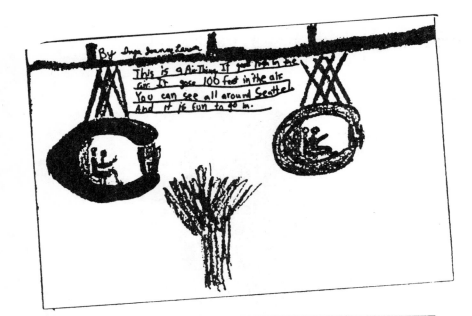

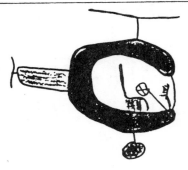

This is a Helucopter. I have bin in a
arplan but not in a Helucopter. I wood
like to go up in one and see all
the butons. A Helucopter is not
like a arplan. A Helucopter dose not
have wing like a arplan. It only has
perpder and best of all I thingk its net.

Christy N.

in the Oldne days Thir
were pepol. They Did not
Have Truks They Did not
Have cars The Had cards.

"Here is a letter. What can you build with this letter?" These samples of first-grade work show some of the possibilities:

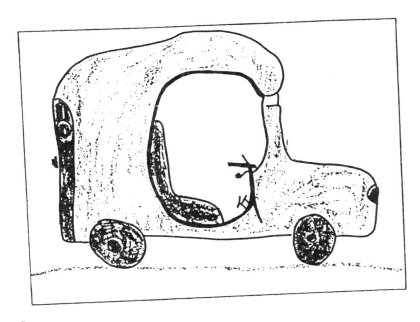

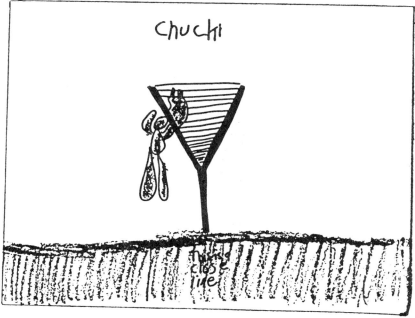

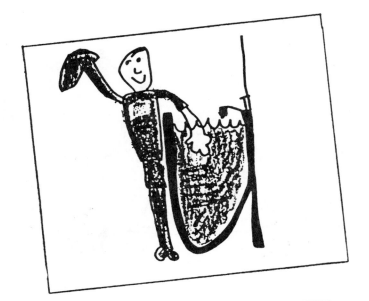

The teacher of a second-grade class collected a box of scraps from a project that used colored construction paper. The children looked at twenty to thirty of the scraps and discussed what they saw in each one. Then each chose a scrap and created a picture and story.

This is Rabbit a Good one to This
rabbit hops arouesd to a Plase
This Rabbit Kaows a lut Of
Things He Kaows weat
2+2 is 4 and Kaows
Weat 4+4 is 8 and I Kaow
You like Rabbits I
like then my Salf I tikg
They are good Pets N Ihave

This is my robut he is on the
Lot I am on the Rat. he
will do and nee thing for
me. he will get cdde
for me. to hes name is
wof.

Inga   He saved 1000,500 people.
This is batman,
This batman can
fly. His real name
is SOPER
DOPFR BATMAN.
200 of them were Kidnapt. 500 were drounding 1000 were wipded.

Inga

This is a man siting on a
stool it is moning time he is
cooking his brefest he is haveing
eggs he was   hikeing and
stade over night his name
is Joe he liks to camp he
is happy he wiligo home
to moro.

Art is an expression of emotion as well as ideas. Much of what children want to express is directly related to their feelings. Creative drama is a fine way to help children to think about facial expressions, body gestures, and posture as expressions of feelings, moods, and ideas.

As children dramatize anger, fear, love, happiness, etc., they can become aware of changing facial characteristics and body positions. This awareness can be transferred to their drawing through questioning by the teacher while moving around the room as the children are working:

"How does the boy in your picture feel?"

"How would he stand if he were angry?"

"How might you stand and look if you were mad at me?"

The expressions in children's art work can be very telling, delightful, and highly communicative, even when their production shows immature coordination or poor control of small muscles. Many of the illustrations in this book reflect this high level of ability to communicate and a much lower level of ability to coordinate and produce exactly.

Certain types of art--paper or wood construction, clay modeling, dioramas, etc.--lend themselves readily to another type of thinking. The child is asked how he made his project. Sequencing is important in this response. A child's responses may be recorded one to a page, sequenced, illustrated, and used as a how-to-do-it book by another child.

With each of these activities, the teacher has a culminating activity for the whole class. The children display their work for each other, and they discuss and share each other's work. Frequently the culminating activity is a class-produced book of art and writing, or just a book of writings. The work is shared orally with the whole class, and each child becomes a teacher for the moment as he reads his page or paragraph or sentence to the class--and as he responds to questions and comments about his work. This sharing of ideas and of responses to ideas is vital in developing a child's inner motivation to learn.

4. Sensory areas.

The teacher discusses and lists the five major senses through which we learn. (There are, of course, a number of other senses, such as the sense of balance, for example.) The teacher sets up five sensory areas, labeling each. There is an area labeled *TOUCH*, one labeled *SEE*, one labeled *HEAR*, one labeled *TASTE*, and one labeled *SMELL*.

Sensory areas are formed with hula hoops or ropes, which allow for intersecting sets. The children are asked to bring small objects and to tell in what sensory area the object fits best. Why? The teacher provokes thought and discussion about each object.

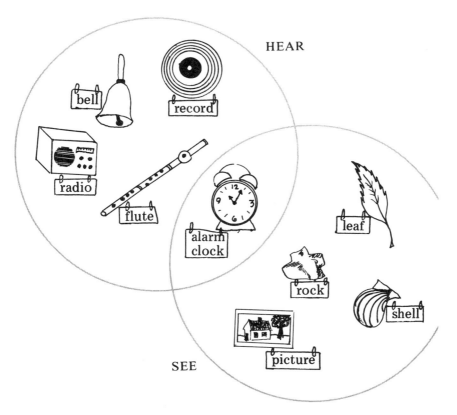

An alarm clock will fit into both the *HEAR* and *SEE* sets if the children decide that it belongs in both, or if they cannot decide in which it belongs. The use of movable circular boundaries for sets permits overlapping so that the alarm clock can fit in both areas simultaneously. This concept of fit or set and overlapping (intersecting sets) is very important to a child's thinking, particularly in mathematics.

Does a flower belong in *SMELL* or *SEE*? Does an apple belong in *SMELL* or *SEE* or *TASTE*? As the children classify and justify their classifications, there will be many arguments as to the best placement. This will provoke thinking and discussion. An important part of concept development is classification--the discrimination of likenesses and differences.

The objects should be labeled with their names. The labels should be affixed loosely so that they can be removed regularly and replaced as children learn to recognize the words.

The teacher may wish to make five scrapbooks, one for each sense. The children classify small objects or pictures. The *TOUCH* book can have objects and materials that have a distinctive feel, such as a piece of sandpaper, a pin, a piece of cloth, etc. Sentences can be written on the pages:

"This feels rough."
"This feels smooth."
"This feels sharp."
"This feels scratchy."

Each sentence begins identically and is completed with a single word elicited from a child. The frame "This feels _____." is repeated throughout the *TOUCH* book so the child can read a book with ease as he learns these two words in a meaningful context.

The *SEE* book may elicit describing words or names:

"It looks _____."
"I see a _____."

Other sensory books may repeat different frames:

"It sounds _____."
"It tastes _____."
"It smells _____."
"The _____ looks _____."
"The _____ tastes _____." etc.

The class newspaper can be a daily activity and can be used to highlight the sensory areas for several weeks. It may be used for homework. Many young children feel proud to have assignments: "Your assignment for homework is to hear something as you walk to school in the morning."

As the children enter class, each is queried, "What did you hear on the way to school?" The answers will range from the commonplace to the poetic:

"I heard a car horn."

"I heard a worm squirming."

"I heard a goose honking as it called to the fall."

On chart paper the teacher records thirty to forty hearings, using each child's name to begin his sentence:

"Tom heard a car horn."

"Mary heard a worm squirming."

"James heard a goose honking as it called to the fall."

Each child will know his line. Each child will begin to recognize the names of his classmates. Each child will have the opportunity to learn thirty to forty sentences. Some will learn them all; some will learn only their own and will forget it by afternoon. Each child will see the repetition of *heard* and *a*.

The newspaper is sent home at the end of the day with some pupil, or each child may take home his own sentence strip. The assignment for the next day is to hear something else on the way to school, to taste something for breakfast, etc.

Of course, the class newspaper is not limited to single-sentence expressions of sensory responses. It should grow throughout each year to become the vehicle for recording news, art, poems, activities, want ads, etc. Children in the first grade are capable of writing or typing imperfectly on ditto masters. With a pupil editorial staff, a weekly newspaper is feasible--or a monthly magazine in which the *Best of Room 22* is featured.

Distributed publications make children very aware of usage and spelling because the children want their work to be correct. The teacher does not need to, and should not, serve as editor. The authors have found that these pupil-produced publications sell the program to parents, as well as making children interested in, and conscious of, writing for others. (It is important, however, that the children do not concentrate on mechanics when writing creatively. The attention to mechanics should *follow* the creation, not accompany it.)

5. **Seasonal areas.**

The various seasons lend themselves to the development of seasonal themes. The theme may center on autumn, winter, spring, or some special holiday season such as Christmas.

Christmas Theme. Begin Christmas through the senses:

"What do we see at Christmas?"   ⎫ Let children
"What do we hear at Christmas?"   ⎪ bring objects
"What do we smell at Christmas?"   ⎬ and cut out
"What do we touch at Christmas?"   ⎪ pictures from
"What do we taste at Christmas?"   ⎭ magazines.

Allow the children to sort both pictures and objects into sensory classifications. Discuss whether each picture or object is best observed, recognized, or understood through seeing, hearing, smelling, touching, or tasting. Dual or multiple classification is almost always possible. The arguments provoked by disagreements can be very valuable if they are used to develop logical thinking.

Make charts with the pictures:

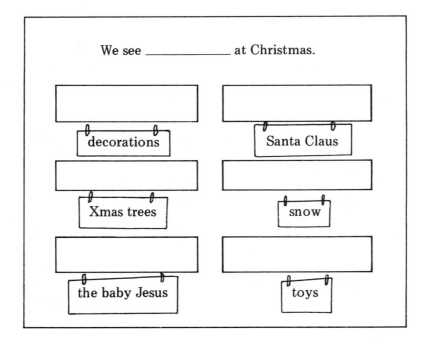

Put labels on with paper clips so that the labels can be removed, jumbled, and replaced by the children. Gain *all* words and pictures from the children.

Oral discussion *first* is a must, followed then by the finding, labeling, and discussing of pictures. The children should be actively engaged in making the charts, deciding on each label, and deciding how many words should go on each label. (The children should watch the teacher print the label.) Stress length of words and any letters the children know to emphasize the phonics that has been taught. (*See Chapter Three.*)

When charts have been made on all senses, begin a Christmas book for each child. The children may use a page for each sense or question. Let them draw in their books small pictures of things they see at Christmas. Then have the children caption each picture. The children may use a sentence frame if they wish: "I see a _____ at Christmas." Follow the same procedure for the other major senses.

Other Christmas ideas to go from discussion into art and writing:
1. "What do you want for Christmas?"
2. "What don't you want for Christmas?"
3. "If you had one hundred dollars, what would you buy? For whom?"
4. "If you were Santa Claus, what would you do?"
5. "If you were Rudolph, what would you do?"
6. "If you were a Christmas tree, how would you feel before Christmas? after Christmas? Why?"
7. "If a box under the tree is round, what might be in it? What would you do with this?"
8. "If a box under the tree is square, what might be in it? What would you do with this?"
9. "If a box under the tree had holes in the top, what might be in it? What would you do with this?"
10. "What would you like that's very big? Why?"
11. "What would you like that's very small? Why?"
12. "What would you like in the bottom of your stocking?"
13. "How does Santa get down the chimney?"

14. "Why does Santa wear a red suit?"
15. "How would you feel if your tummy shook like a bowlful of jelly?"

After building and expanding these thoughts orally, the children may draw or express their thoughts creatively and then state their thoughts in written words. Some may need to dictate their thoughts. Others might use a sentence frame such as "I want a _____ for Christmas because _____."

6. Pictures.

Single pictures or groups of related pictures may be used to evoke discussion. Groups of pictures may be sequenced to tell a whole story, but a single picture may be more effective because it requires more imagination.

The teacher must first set the scene. "Somebody took this picture with his camera. Something may have happened to make the photographer want to take this picture. Something may have happened after he took the picture. What do you think may have happened before the picture was taken? Why do you think the photographer took the picture? What is happening in the picture? What may have happened after the picture was taken?" One picture may have a hundred beginnings and a hundred endings.

If one child makes up a story about the picture, the teacher questions the listeners to develop the three areas of comprehension: thinking skills, empathy, and vocabulary.

7. Nursery rhymes, poetry, and stories.

One of the most important things a teacher can do is to read to children. Through this medium, the child hears and becomes familiar with standard literary English. He learns to listen and think and become part of the story. He learns to react to an author's thoughts, to offer opinions of his own, and to expand both his own thinking and that of his classmates. He learns to enjoy good literature and to value the ideas of others.

When the teacher reads aloud to develop thinking skills, there is no need for ability grouping. The children may be grouped into discussion-size groups of ten or twelve, but the groups do not need to be given the stultifying labels of "able," "average," and "dull."

Practicing the skills of drawing conclusions or making inferences is not dependent upon word-recognition skill; thinking skills can be practiced at a much higher level than that dictated by word recognition.

This freedom from ability grouping benefits children at all levels of ability. It also benefits the teacher because the thinking skill discussions are lively and stimulating. (The circling of the right answer on a workbook-type exercise following the reading of a paragraph is rarely stimulating to either the teacher or the children.)

Nursery rhymes. Nursery rhymes can be used effectively as lessons in reading. Many children can recite the words before they come to school, even though they know little or nothing of the verses' meanings. Some nursery rhymes are, of course, mostly nonsense, but nursery rhymes afford a good opportunity for children to begin thinking about the written word and to provide enjoyable answers to questions about meaning.

The teacher starts by printing a nursery rhyme, such as "Little Bo Peep," on a chart or the chalkboard. The children then "read" and "reread" the rhyme. They are helped to enjoy the words and the rhythm, and they sing, clap, and dance to the rhythm of the rhyme.

Then the teacher asks a very simple question, such as "Where could Little Bo Peep's sheep have gone? Remember that no one could find them." This question, though simple, requires thinking.

This question also requires an oral answer that will usually contain a preposition, and children need a great deal of help in understanding prepositions. The answers will begin in many ways if the children are encouraged to expand each other's thoughts:

> "behind the barn"
> "over the hill"
> "under the bridge"
> "around the mountain"
> "beside the garage" etc.

After eliciting responses from the children and encouraging individually different responses, the teacher leads the children to discuss their answers and tries to expand the children's thinking. Not all responses can be expanded, but many of them can be, and these responses deserve to be carried further. Take the children as far as they will go. Encourage the children to save their wonderful thoughts on paper so that they can have their good thinking to enjoy for a long time. This can be done easily in two ways.

1. Sheets of 9" x 12" newsprint are passed out and folded in half. Each child draws his thought on one half of the paper, and the teacher takes individual dictation and prints on the other half.

The paper may then be folded closed, and the title of the nursery rhyme printed on the front cover. These little individual books may either be added to the classroom library or taken home.

2. As the children respond orally to the question, the teacher prints their responses on the chalkboard. After all responses are elicited, the children read their own responses. Each child copies his own response onto a sheet of paper and draws a picture to illustrate it. The sheets may be fastened together, and a classbook entitled *Our Thoughts about Little Bo Peep's Sheep* may be added to the library.

Additional nursery rhymes and questions that have been used successfully are the following:

"Where, Oh Where, Has My Little Dog Gone?"
  ("Where has her dog gone?")
"A-Hunting We Will Go"
  ("How would you catch a fox?")
"Jack, Be Nimble"
  ("Why would anyone want to jump over a candlestick?")
"Little Jack Horner"
  ("Why was he in a corner?")
"Humpty Dumpty"
  ("Why did Humpty Dumpty climb the wall? How did he get up on that wall?")

Poetry. Poetry should be read often. Children love to hear and feel the rhythm. They like to know a poem well enough so that they can chant it with their teacher. They love the feel of some of the words, and they like to repeat these words over and over again. Poetry provides many opportunities to increase the child's interest in words and thoughts.

After reading poetry, the teacher asks the children about the words. "Were there any words that you liked? Why? Was it the way the words sounded or the way the words made you feel? How would you use these words? Could the words be used in any other way?"

The teacher should make a chart of the words that the children liked. The children should be asked to pick out words with terminal rhyme and words with initial rhyme (words that start the same).

The children should also discuss the characters or thoughts and feelings in a poem:

"How does this poem make you feel? Why?"

"What caused the feeling? Was it the rhythm, or the thoughts, or both?"

"What other kinds of thoughts could be told in this rhythm?"

Have the children write their own poems. Begin simply with couplets that they can complete orally:

Animals _____ Children_____
                        or
Adults _____ Children_____

Expand these couplets to triplets and gradually omit the beginnings so that the children complete the thoughts in a frame, first orally, and then in writing:

Couplets

_____   _____

_____   _____

Triplets

_____   _____

_____   _____

_____   _____

Cinquain poetry is fun for children in the primary grades. The frame is as follows:

_____ (one word giving the title)
_____ _____ (two words describing the title)
_____ _____ _____ (three words expressing an action
of the title)
_____ _____ _____ _____ (four words expressing a
feeling of the title)
_____ (a synonym for the title)

The following are examples written by first-grade children:

Johnny Cash
Actor, TV
Sings on TV
He feels happy today
Man!

Squirrel
Very beautiful
It eats peanuts
It feels wild no
Sissy

Toad
Green, slippery
Hops on you
It feels slippery, slushy
Frog

Turtle
Hard shell
Swims in water
Is afraid of people
Tortoise.

Teacher
Very nice
She can teach
She is very cuddly
Mommy

A third-grade teacher gave the following report of a poetry project that lasted just a little more than a month:

Our project--a poetry booklet to give to our mothers on Mother's Day.

To set the mood, I read to the class one of Dr. Seuss's stories, which is just full of rhyming words, explaining that stories can be written in poetry, adding interest and rhythm to the story.

We perused our language book and read many of the short poems, noting the way poetry looks, with its pattern of lines. We discussed the reasons why we liked poetry, such as how the ear catches the rhythm and rhyme, how it stirs one's imagination and brings to one's mind the feeling of what the poem is expressing.

Our first attempt at writing poetry was done by the class as a whole. I wrote the first line on the board and from there on the pupils did the rest. One of the biggest problems encountered was that the pupils would often suggest nonsensical lines in order to get the last word to rhyme. Rhyming took precedence over thought.

I found the pupils most interested in this project and spurred their interest further by reading each

poem to the class. Some days I might receive four or
maybe just one from the class. The project could not
be rushed nor was too much pressure used for fear of
instilling a dislike for poetry. Praise was given for the
least effort.

The pupils enjoyed seeing their verses in print
and had to read the verse before the proper illustration was drawn.

I am sure the mothers of the third-grade class will
cherish their gift of poems for years to come.

This teacher would not accept just anything and required
several children to rewrite their poems two or three times.
The rewriting always followed individual discussion with the
pupil. Sometimes a pupil asked for help from other children
in the class.

Twenty-four of the twenty-eight children created poems.
Four typical poems are quoted here:

Easter is not far away,
I hope it's not a gloomy day,
A rabbit that brings eggs is a gas.
I wonder how he'll cross Agate Pass.

Summer, beautiful summer
That's when plants do grow
Winter after winter
That's when it rains and snows.

I saw a star slide down the sky,
Going fast as it went by,
Too lovely to be sold
And too hot to hold
Good to make a wish on
And then forever to be gone

When the sky was blue
And grass, trees and wild flowers grew?
Remember birds and frogs and ants?
Remember when earth had a chance?

Stories. All teachers read stories to their pupils--books that
the teacher knows and enjoys. This enjoyment is imperative
because the teacher's attitude is conveyed to the children.

Both teachers and pupils derive great pleasure from sharing books that the teacher reads. By reading to children, we teach them that books are to be enjoyed. We teach them how to enjoy a book, and we provide a major opportunity for the children to learn standard English.

Activities to help children enjoy books.

1. In very simple books, the teacher hesitates before saying a key word or phrase, and the children frequently supply the word or phrase. In books with much repetition, the teacher also allows the children to supply the repeated words. Supplying the words helps to give children the feeling that reading is easy--rather like talking.

2. Make a list of phrases from stories that interest children. They may choose descriptive phrases or alliterative phrases:
   "as tiny as"
   "so quiet that"
   "the great grey-green, greasy Limpopo River."
   Build enjoyment with the alliterative phrases. Discuss the mood the alliteration evokes. "How do these words make you feel? Would there be something nice or something nasty in the great grey-green, greasy Limpopo River? What might it be?" Have the children use the phrases orally in completing a frame sentence such as:
   "I saw _____ in the great grey-green, greasy Limpopo River."

   The following examples were written by third-grade children, stimulated by reading Robert McCloskey's *Time of Wonder* and by discussion of McCloskey's phrase ". . .so quiet that you can hear. . .the sound of growing ferns, pushing aside dead leaves, unrolling their fiddleheads, slowly unfurling, slowly stretching." Note the alliteration and descriptive language used in their writing.

Mike

It was so quiet that I could here the wind dancing with the leaves in the trees.

It was so quiet that I could here Bolas Spider playing in the breeze.

It was quiet I heard the honey bees dancing.

Stacey

It is so quiet thet I could hear quietness of the beach and the wind playing with the water.

In the forest I could hear the birds singing and the deer running through the forest and the beautiful sound of the baby bald eagles crying to their moms.

Kim

It was so quiet I could hear the people ecoing. I could smell campfires burning. And the birds chirping. And crickets cricking. And deer running through the woods. The sound of bears rooring like thunder. The rain whispering while it falls to the ground.

Colleen

It was so quiet that I could hear the scamppering of feet on the sand. I could hear the seagulls call. I could hear the waves pounse against the rocks.

I could hear song of the wind.

Brian

It was so quiet that I could hear the sound of nature in the darkness.

I could even hear a crick with fish splashing their wiggly tails.

I could hear the splashing of a waterfall near by. I could hear a breeze whistling throgh the grass.

3. Make lists of interesting ways stories begin or end. Use these lists to assist children in writing and telling their own stories. Many of these ways can be found by having children refer to their favorite books. One teacher used the phrase "just right," developed the

concept by personal example, and discussed what things were just right for the children in the class. After full oral development, one child wrote the following delightful story. (Many other children in this first-grade class wrote equally well.)

Just right
Cuddly Cozy warm Just right
for me and mommy. his name is Jimmy.
he likes Mrs. Chiba. I do to. he is four
he will be five soon. he has a dog.
I have a bird. his dogs Name is laddy.
Jimmy has the same colour hair as me. He is
my brother.

4. Children's books deserve much discussion. The ideas need expansion. The teacher should personally react to the authors' ideas and should elicit personal responses from the children. The example of reaction by the teacher is important in initiating this type of discussion, but the children should not be trained to parrot the teacher's reactions. Diversity of reaction should be encouraged. One teacher read Ruth Krauss's *A Hole Is to Dig* to a first-grade class. The class spent forty to fifty minutes discussing various types of holes. With well over one hundred ideas in the air, the children created thirty-four individual responses, with no two responses even remotely alike (except for the idea of "hole"). Following are five of the responses:

A hole is to put a fence post in. Linda

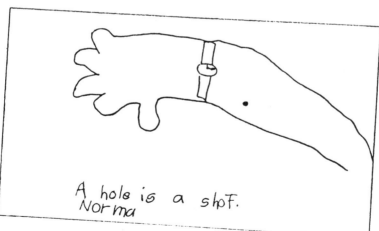

A hole is a shot. Norma

5. Creative dramatics is a wonderful way to make a story live for children. The authors' experiences demonstrate the power of using this approach. They have revisited several classrooms one to two years after dramatizing a story with children, and are remembered by those children, not by their own names but by the title of the story that was dramatized.

Creative dramatics allows children to recall story events, characters, and plot in sequence. It allows for empathy and encourages the reuse and the learning of vocabulary used in the story. This is a very natural way to foster the growth of thinking skills.

The authors have found that many children need assistance in beginning dramatization and have found it helpful to have the class as a whole practice being a single character. Inhibition is lost in the crowd as teacher and children copy each other.

The Five Chinese Brothers[3] shows how a simple story can be used to broaden the child's understanding of character and plot. First, the teacher reads the story orally. Then the teacher asks the pupils to be the various characters.

"Let's all be the first Chinese brother. What do you remember about him?"

(The first Chinese brother is the one who swallowed the sea.)

"Good! Let's all swallow the sea. How do you feel? How do you look?" etc.

Next, the teacher asks the children to be the executioner.

"I want all of these people (indicating about half the class) to be the executioner. What will you do? Good! Show me how you will do that."

Dramatize with the children, helping them to become the executioner. Then go on to the second Chinese brother.

"Now I want the rest of the class to be the second Chinese brother. How do you remember him?"

(He is the one with the iron neck.)

"Show me."

Have the children face each other in two lines, the executioners in one line and the second Chinese brothers in the other.

"Now, executioners, chop off their heads! What happens? How do you executioners feel? How do you Chinese brothers feel?"

The teacher asks questions to develop an awareness of the different characters, of feelings, of situations, and of predictable outcomes. The teacher encourages the pupils to use their entire bodies, helping them to empathize fully with the character, showing their thoughts and feelings in voice and gesture. This will carry over into oral reading, and it will be reflected in their comprehension in both oral and silent reading.

The teacher should play out many situations with the entire class. Creativity and responses are easier to elicit with the many actors in the entire class working together rather than individually.

After the children have responded as groups, they should be ready to take individual parts and put on a play. Allow the children to choose what character they want to be, but insist that they be able to tell *who* they are and *what* they are going to do before they can participate. This will encourage good listening habits and fuller participation in future activities.

6. Discuss the author's message with the class. "Is it the same for everyone? Why? Why not? Did someone feel something different?" Allow the children to express their ideas and bring their own backgrounds into the stories. Teach them to understand and accept each other's ideas and the reasons for these ideas.

7. Help children to become aware of an author's style. Most children enjoy the style of Dr. Seuss, and they should gain some understanding of this style. See if you can help them to imitate it. Many other authors, too, have a distinctive style, with which children can become familiar.

The following example is a class story written by a first-grade class. The teacher had enjoyed reading Rudyard Kipling's *Just So Stories* to the class. Because the teacher enjoyed the stories so much, the children loved these stories. They asked if they could write a *Just So* story themselves. In fact, they wrote two such stories, one of which was "How the Skunk Got His Smell." (Note that the children have imitated Kipling's alliteration, his use of "Oh Best Beloved," and his repetition.)

"How the Skunk Got His Smell"
Written by First Grade
(We made it up)
Illustrated by First grade
(We made the pictures)

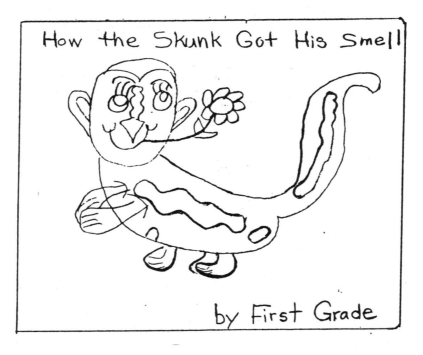

Long ago, deep in the woods, Oh Best Beloved, the skunk had no smell.

There was a skunk named Silly, Sassy, Skippy Skunk. He had a bad habit. He ate everything he smelled. He would eat and he would eat and he would eat, eat, eat, EAT! Everytime he ate, he got spanked. He got spanked and he got spanked and he spanked, spanked, spanked, SPANKED! Everytime he got spanked he got mad. He got mad and he got mad and he got mad, mad, mad, MAD!

One day Silly, Sassy, Skippy Skunk smelled a spray can. He ate it whole. Then he got spanked by his father, spanked by his mother, spanked by his aunts, uncles, sisters and brother. He was mad.

Then he smelled a skunk cabbage. He ate it. Then he got spanked by his father, spanked by his mother, spanked by his aunts, uncles, sisters and brother. He was mad.

Then he smelled something in Mr. McGregor's garden. So he went under the fence and ate a whole field of onions and garlic!

Now the more he ate, Oh Best Beloved, the more stuck the spray can got. Then most of what he ate went into the spray can. The can was full of skunk cabbage, onions, and garlic!

Now it happened whenever he was spanked, it set off the spray can. So when he was spanked by his father, spanked by his mother, spanked by his aunts, uncles, sisters and brother, they all got sprayed. Then THEY got mad and they got mad, mad, mad, MAD! So they never spanked him again.

"Where did you get that smell?" they all asked. Then all the skunks went out to get a smell. From that day to this, Oh Best Beloved, all the skunks have a smell that they can use when they get mad or spanked.

To summarize--this chapter has dealt with communication and stimulating children's thinking.

The RIOTT program is teacher-motivated and structured, yet it is individualized and educationally open. (*See Chapter Six for a discussion of open education.*) Most of the teaching is done by the teacher working with the entire class, stimulating the children and provoking ideas. But most of the responding is done individually, and it is open. The children's responses are different individual contributions to themes and to the intellectual content of the classroom.

The authors believe that this kind of teaching and learning is both practical, workable, and yet truly individualized. Children have almost total freedom in what they say and how they respond. But the children must respond, and this requirement leads them into making significant choices.

Most classes that follow this type of program become environmentally and behaviorally open, but there is never any question about who has the ultimate responsibility. It is the teacher's responsibility to make sure that significant learning is taking place--that children are learning to think, to communicate, to listen, to speak, to write, and to read.

Chapter III

AWARENESS *of* SOUND

A typical definition of *phonics* is "the phonetic rudiments used in teaching reading and pronunciation." But phonics is more than that. Phonics embraces all language arts skills, such as *speaking, listening,* and *writing* skills.

Spoken language is made up of sounds. These sounds are limited in number and contrast with each other. They are repeated in varying combinations to make different words. These different sounds of speech are called phonemes.* Phonemes in English are represented by one or more letters. Accordingly, children have to become aware of the alphabetic nature of their written language. The authors have found that this awareness develops naturally if children are taught how to listen to speech and how to recognize phonemes by writing. This is an *encoding* process.

Children who first learn encoding make a very natural transition to pronouncing words, which is *decoding*. The authors' experience indicates that children who are taught phonics through decoding rarely learn to write as a natural transition, and many have great difficulty in applying phonics to reading.

---

*A large technical literature exists in linguistics on the concept of a phoneme. The word is used in this book to mean the least difference in sound by which one word is differentiated from another. There are both consonant and vowel phonemes. We tell the words *pat* and *bat* apart by distinguishing the consonant phonemes /p/ and /b/; we tell the words *pat* and *pit* apart by distinguishing the vowel phonemes /a/ and /i/. Phonemes are traditionally written between slashes.

A teacher must be keenly aware of the phonemic quality of spoken language and must recognize the repetition of phonemes in spoken language. This is essential because the teacher has to help the children to develop phonemic awareness.

In written language, each phoneme is represented by a letter or a combination of letters. The principle of alphabetic writing is maintained if each phoneme of the spoken language is represented by one or more letters. It does not matter that different letters may be used to represent a particular phoneme, e.g., *c* and *k* for /*k*/ -- nor does it matter that a single letter may be used to represent two or more phonemes, e.g., *c* for /*k*/ and /*s*/ or that a letter may represent no phonemes, e.g., *e* in *like*, or that two letters may stand for a single phoneme, e.g., *ch* for /č/. The spellings of *cite*, *site*, and *sight* are alphabetic in principle.

Almost all children hear the *differences* between similar words. Children do not mistake *cat* and *cap* when asked to point to the picture of one or the other. Similarly, children have no difficulty in distinguishing *cup* from *cap*, nor *bat* from *cat*. The words *cat* and *cap* constitute a "minimal pair." They are wholly alike except for a single phoneme, /*t*/ in the case of *cat* and /*p*/ in the case of *cap*. The minimal pair in *bat/cat* is /*b*/ and /*k*/ represented by *c* in spelling. The concept of "minimal pair" is one by which linguists isolate phonemes and is also a useful classroom technique in teaching and identifying phonemes.

Many children, however, do not hear the *likenesses* in such minimal pairs as *cat* and *cap*, *cup* and *cap*, and *bat* and *cat*. Each of these words has three phonemes--two that are similar and one that is different in each pair of words.

Children must learn to hear the phonemes of their spoken language--to recognize the likenesses, as well as the differences--if they are to understand the alphabetic principle of English spelling and writing, and if they are to understand and recognize spelling patterns.

Since we use the twenty-six-letter Roman alphabet to write English and since there are more than forty phonemes in spoken English, some letters or combinations of letters of the alphabet have to be used to represent more than one phoneme. (Linguists do not agree about the precise number of phonemes in English.)

This causes difficulty for children when they are learning how to read, because the irregular spellings obscure the alphabetic nature of our spelling and writing system. The confusion is increased if a child begins reading simple material before he has learned to *hear* the phonemes of his spoken language.

Many children never understand that writing is listening to and identifying phonemes and representing these phonemes in sequence with letters. As a result, many children never realize that the word-recognition part of the reading process is a reversal of the writing process--an identifying of the letters and the phonemes they represent.

Children who fail to grasp this understanding remain poor spellers, and by the third grade they have developed most or all of the symptoms characteristic of dyslexia. They have become "remedial readers." This tragedy can be avoided if the teacher provides instruction that enables children to learn the principle of alphabetic writing.

1. Knowing what a word is.

When we speak, our language is a fairly steady flow. Each consonant acts as an interruption, but each succeeding vowel continues the flow of sound.

As we speak, we pause to show meaning; we pause as we cluster words into meaningful phrases. In writing, we attempt to encode these pauses with periods, commas, or other punctuation marks.

The breaks that we *think* we hear between words that we signify by spaces in our writing and printing do not represent pauses in our speaking. These spaces are an artificial contrivance of our writing system, learned by noting the repetitiveness of sound groups (words) in oral speech. We "hear" the spaces because we know each word and we know what a word is.

Say the sentence "The cat came home." Note that you make no real stops between *the* and *cat*, *cat* and *came*, or *came* and *home*. Yet you know this is a sentence containing four words.

But what is a word? Say the word *preposition*. Note that you make no real pause between syllables. To someone not knowing any English, *preposition* would sound as much like a four-word sentence as "The cat came home" does. To a child of five or six, "In a right-angled triangle, the square of the hypotenuse equals the sum of the squares of the other two sides" sounds as nonsensical as "supercalifragilisticexpialido-cious."

To tell a child that "a word is a sound or combination of sounds that functions as the smallest meaningful unit of language when used in isolation" is of no help whatsoever. Yet a child must come to understand what a word is. He must learn to discriminate words from syllables, and he must learn to hear the phonemes in both words and syllables.

The beginning writing of young children reflects their difficulty in recognizing words. Children often write without leaving any space between words. If we approach the problem of spacing as a writing problem and badger children to leave "two fingers" between words, we may be overlooking the real problem. The real problem is to teach children to *hear* words, to recognize the differences between words and nonwords, and *then* to learn the convention of word spacing.

The teacher can develop this awareness of words by short daily oral drills. Using normal speech, the teacher says sentences such as the following:

"The cat came home."

"How are you?"

"When did you go to bed last night?"

"I like Halloween."

After each sentence, the teacher asks, "How many words did I say?"

There will usually be a variety of responses because the children confuse words, syllables, and phrases in normal speech. The teacher may then have the children repeat the sentence in unison. As the children speak in unison, there is a natural slowing-down that emphasizes each word.

The chalkboard may be used to develop the concept that our spoken language can be symbolized. As the children say a sentence, the teacher makes a mark for each word. Then the teacher writes the words under the marks so that children can see the words and the spacing. For example, as the children say "How are you?" the teacher marks and then writes

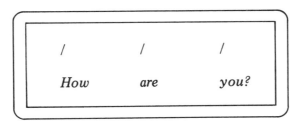

The teacher does this with many sentences, always relating the speech to the writing.

The concept that speech can be symbolized needs reinforcement, which may be achieved in several ways. The children may look in books, magazines, and newspapers to observe the following:

> spacing
> number of words on a line
> some words printed in italics or capitals because the author wanted to say that word "louder" to emphasize it
> different type faces.

Children love to cut out samples of different type faces and paste these in their notebooks.

When reading stories to the children, the teacher may wish to point out type variations. As the children begin to dictate stories, and later begin to write, the concept is reinforced and retaught individually. Some children will need continued practice in distinguishing words for a year or more. *(See pp. 81-85 for an example of this in children's writing.)*

2. **Sensing the relationship between the length of the spoken word and the written word.**

   In beginning to relate the spoken word and the written word, the teacher first relates the length of the written word to the length of the spoken word. (Other sound-symbol relationships are taught later.) The teacher has the children think of short words and long words. As the children say the words, the teacher writes the words on the chalkboard, so that the children may see the lengths. The teacher says:

"It took a short time to say *cat*."

"Look how short the written word *cat* is."

"It took a much longer time to say *hippopotamus*."

"Look how long the written word *hippopotamus* is."

The teacher should have the children say a number of sentences (which may flow naturally from class discussion). For example, Bill might say, "I saw an enormous dog on the way to school." Then the teacher would say, "Mary, Bill said, 'I saw an enormous dog on the way to school.' Tell me a little word that Bill said."

The teacher writes Mary's response and asks, "Tom, what is the biggest word you hear in 'I saw an enormous dog on the way to school'?" The teacher elicits and writes *enormous*.

The teacher always says each word in isolation while drawing the comparison between spoken length and written length. (The children should, of course, understand that they are learning a generality, to which there are exceptions.)

3. **Becoming aware of the likenesses in words.**

Almost all children beginning school react meaningfully to minute differences in spoken language. This can be demonstrated simply. Show a child two pictures, one of a cap and one of a cup. Say to the child, "Point to the picture of the cap." Most children will respond correctly. Say, "Point to the picture of the cup." Again most children will respond correctly.

In saying each sentence, the teacher utters approximately twenty phonemes (the number depending on the counting system). In each of these two sentences, there are nineteen like phonemes and one that is different. The children respond to that one difference.

Some children may hear the two sentences as two long words. Most children will not be aware of the like phonemes they have heard. Most will not know that they have heard six words in each sentence which were the same and one word in each which was different.

Lack of awareness of phonetic likenesses is relatively unimportant in the oral functioning of the children. But this hearing skill must be developed if children are to write and read. Children must learn to hear likenesses in speech, even though hearing likenesses is much more difficult than hearing differences.

4. Encoding spoken language.

There are many ways to teach children to hear phonemes, but the most efficient and productive way is to teach children to write (encode) their thoughts. This requires the child to think--to put his idea into words (in sentences), to identify each word, to analyze each word into phonemes, and to represent these phonemes in sequence.

To get children to write, we teach them to hear words, to listen for the phonemes in words, and to know the letters that are usually used to represent the phonemes.

The child must be inducted gradually into writing. He is expected to encode as much of each word as possible. Conventional spelling is *not* expected as children begin to write. The children simply write what they hear, as best they can.

If conventional spelling is required initially, the program will fail, because the children will be inhibited from expressing their ideas in writing. They will fail to learn the alphabetic principle of written English, because conventional spelling obscures the sound-letter relationships. (In one first-grade class observed by the authors, a boy wrote *helucopter* instead of *helicopter.* Nine of the ten letters were correct, yet by traditional grading *helucopter* would be marked 100 percent wrong.)

When spelling phonetically, the child practices or drills himself meaningfully on all the phonics he has been taught. He should not be chastised for not knowing what he has not been taught, nor should he be restricted in his communication to those words he can spell correctly.

Children know that they are learning; children know that their first attempts at spelling are guesses, approximations. There is no danger that a child will drill his mistakes; he knows that he still must learn conventional spelling. He will learn conventional spelling from his reading of books; the words he uses in writing are repeated and repeated in the books he reads. He will also learn conventional spelling when it is specifically taught later. And, of course, he will learn conventional spelling as he refines his auditory skill and combines this with his knowledge of spelling patterns.

In the RIOTT program, each child is taught to write--to encode his spoken language. Four things are taught simultaneously for each letter of the alphabet:

1. the name of the letter
2. the sound (phoneme) the letter represents*
3. the feel of each phoneme as it is pronounced
4. the way to write each letter.

In one first-grade class following the RIOTT program, the teacher had used a number of the suggestions given thus far, had talked with the children about one letter, and had begun with the **Myself** theme, introducing the words *I* and *like*. On the sixth day of school, the teacher and children discussed "things that children like" and "things that children like to do."

The teacher expected that the children would use the word *I* and draw a picture to finish their thoughts. But the teacher got some pleasant surprises. A boy named Byron, whose reading readiness test indicated low-average ability, produced the following paper:

---

*Step 2 is a most troublesome area. Consonants, by their very definition (*con--with; sonus--sound*), are those phonemes which cannot be vocalized without the addition of a vowel. Vowels, again by definition, are noises or vocalizations which can be made independently. The part of phonics which a child needs to learn in order to write and read is only a small part. The child's phonics program in the RIOTT program is a listening and then a writing program. A child learns to hear phonemes in words. He does not start with isolated phonemes and build words. The child's drill as he learns is 99 percent or more with spoken sentences or words which he analyzes auditorily. To teach him to write, the authors do teach that consonants such as *b* say *buh* with as little

When asked to read his thoughts, Byron read as follows:

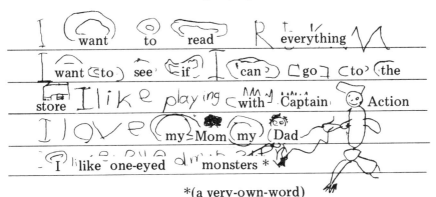

*(a very-own-word)

Note several things about Byron's work:

1. He does not appear to be low-average, and subsequent work throughout the year verified that Byron was unusually gifted and creative.

2. He developed his own code. He used a rebus for the things that could be pictured: an eye for *see*, a sidewalk for *go*, a building for *store*, two hands for *with*, etc. He used mouth shapes for words that could not be pictured, which was ascertained by his own oral description of what he did. (Note particularly the tongue and teeth of *the*.)

3. He demonstrated that he knew what a word is. Each word is represented individually.

4. He gave visual proof of why some of the basic little words, such as *to*, *and*, and *if* are so difficult to learn--they cannot be pictured, and they have no meaning out of context.

---

emphasis on the *uh* as possible. The teaching of all consonants is multisensory, auditory, tactile, visual, and kinesthetic. The authors have found no practical way to remain *both* technically correct and pragmatically successful in teaching consonant sounds. They have found that this technical problem is totally irrelevant to the child's learning to write and read when the phonemes and letters are introduced as described here, and when the practice of isolating phonemes begins with the sentence or the whole word. Children understand and recognize this addition or distortion, and the teacher should acknowledge their understanding. The selection of *s* and *m* as the first two consonants avoids the problem momentarily. However, the /s/ in *soap* is not *s-s-s-soap*, nor is the /m/ in *mother m-m-m-mother*.

5. Furthermore, Byron's work is proof that tests which require motor coordination or drawing skill may underrate intellectually able children if they are used to predict reading readiness.

In teaching letters of the alphabet, the authors suggest beginning with six consonants and a short vowel, then six more consonants with another short vowel. Then complete the consonants and short vowels, the long vowels, the diphthongs, and then an analysis of spelling patterns.

Single-letter representations should be taught before digraphs. Initially, only one phoneme should be taught for each letter, such as the /k/ sound for *c*, even though *c* commonly represents the sound of /s/ and is used with *h* in the /č/ sound in *child*.

Children must recognize and understand the alphabetic principle of our writing system, and this principle is seriously obscured if a one-to-one letter relationship is not maintained in the beginning. (This means, of course, that the teacher initially must accept and even encourage unconventional spellings.)

There is no magic order for teaching the letters, but there are some practical considerations that should be kept in mind: (1) The letters taught first should have a high utility in writing. For example, *s* and *m* are used much more often than *j* and *z*. (2) The letters taught at a particular time should not be too much alike in sound or written formation. Thus *m* and *n* would not be taught together because they are so similar in sound and appearance; *d* and *b* would not be taught together because of their similarity of appearance.

A few sounds should be taught fully to mastery before introducing additional sounds. Children should learn to recognize sounds in beginning, ending, and medial positions within spoken words. Children should also learn to recognize sounds in spoken sentences and phrases.

The teaching of the first letter will take much longer than the teaching of any subsequent letter. The teaching of the first six letters will take much longer than the teaching of any subsequent group. Similarly, the teaching of the first vowel will take longer than any subsequent vowel.

The authors suggest teaching the following consonants first:

s (as in *sat*)	*b*
m	*c* (as in *cat*)
r	*t*

In teaching a consonant that can be sounded in isolation, such as *s*, the teacher writes *s* on the chalkboard and points to it, saying, "This is the letter *s*." Then the teacher makes the following statements:

1. "Its name is *ess*."
2. "It stands for the sound *s-s-s-s*."
3. "You can feel how to make the /s/ sound when you say, 'Simple Simon says sister Sarah sounds silly.' Repeat after me, 'Simple Simon . . . .' What do you do with your lips, your teeth, your tongue, your mouth when you say *ess*?"
4. "You write an *s* like this." (The teacher demonstrates the writing of the letter *s*. At first, lowercase forms are used exclusively.)

Each child should have an individual chalkboard. Each child should copy the *s*. The class should answer in unison as the teacher points to the letter and asks, "What is the name of this letter? What sound does the letter represent?" And each child should write when the teacher says, "Write an *s* on your chalkboard." These three directions are drilled randomly. *S* is taught, say, on Monday, retaught on Tuesday and Wednesday, and reviewed many times thereafter.

In teaching children to write or print, the teacher is guided by one principle. *The child has a thought to convey. He must learn to write legibly enough so that his handwriting does not interfere with someone's reading his message.* The writing of letters is taught simply by having the children watch and copy as the teacher writes on the chalkboard. The authors feel that the children will learn best if they have individual chalkboards on which to practice. A piece of colored construction paper can substitute for a more substantial chalkboard and will last for more than a week. Individual differences in muscular control are best cared for by using unlined paper or chalkboards for most writing. Although this sometimes results in writing going askew or a word being written with letters of varying sizes, it also results in individual letters being more distinctly different. For example, the printed difference between *n* and *h*, or *a* and *d*, is largely how far up the ascending line goes. The authors recently observed a boy diagnosed as cerebral palsied successfully encoding as he scribbled across the blank page. Had he been forced to conform to lines, the task would have been impossible.

The teacher begins reinforcing and using *s* immediately, asking if anyone has an /s/ in his name. Each child says his name, and they all listen for *esses*. If they hear an /s/, they try to identify where they hear the /s/ in the name before the teacher writes the name on the chalkboard.

The teacher works with *Sally* or *Sam* or *Susan* or *Kris* or *Casper*. The teacher ignores the /s/ in the middle of *Susan* unless some child insists that he hears the medial sound of /s/, and at this stage the teacher may accept the /s/ sound as being in the middle of *Susan* since the sounds of /s/ and /z/ are so similar, particularly to the untrained or immature ear.

The teacher calls the children's attention to the letter *s* in each written name and relates it to the /s/ sound that they hear in pronouncing the name. The teacher helps the children perceive the auditory sequence and the consequent written sequence. The auditory analysis of the spoken word should almost always precede the writing or looking at the printed word.

Labels can be used to reinforce the phonics taught. Children can now begin to recognize labels through length of word, and *s* in initial position. As phonetic skill develops, labels can be removed, jumbled, and returned to correct places. This begins the transfer from writing to reading.

The teacher begins an *s* chart or an *s* scrapbook or both. The children locate pictures that, when named, contain the phoneme /s/. Pictures are added daily, with the /s/ phoneme being initial, medial, or terminal. The chart or scrapbook is reviewed regularly.

The teacher says words and phrases, directing the children, "If you hear an /s/ sound when I say *sock* (or *dog*, *post*, or *hippopotamus*, etc.), write an *s* on your chalkboard.

If you do not hear the sound /s/, write nothing on your chalkboard."

Later, the children put two horizontal lines on their chalkboards

and the teacher says, "If you hear an /s/ at the beginning of the word, put an *s* on the first line. If you hear an /s/ at the end of the word, put an *s* on the last line." The teacher illustrates this three or four times. The teacher then dictates *soap, cats, Saturday, hippopotamus,* etc. Much later still, the teacher has the children make three lines and dictates words with the sound of /s/ in initial, medial, and terminal positions.

The teacher has been developing simultaneously the theme **Myself** or some other theme. The children have been talking about likes and dislikes. They have drawn pictures to complete the sentence frame

"I like (   ) "

John has drawn skates. The teacher shares John's sentence and suggests to John, "Can you hear any of the letters that might be used to spell the word *skates*?" The teacher helps John to recognize the initial and final /s/ sound and to write as well as draw.

"I like (🛼🛼) "

When the children share their work, the teacher reviews John's work with the whole class, as well as the work of several other children.

As the children talk about what they like, the teacher may write each of their likes on the chalkboard and ask about each word before writing. "Do you hear an /s/ in the word *singing (sunflower, eating,* etc.)? You can spell part of that word yourself," the teacher says, if the word contains an /s/.

Once the phoneme /s/ has been taught, s is the letter accepted to spell words such as *city, circus, bicycle,* or *receive,* until the spelling principle determining c or s has been taught and the two letters that can represent the phoneme /s/ have been taught.

The teacher teaches m in the same way that s was taught, and then combines both in drills. Most of the drill is oral and requires that the children respond individually on their chalkboards. The teacher says the following:

1. "Does the word *mother* begin with an s or an m?"
                sister
                matter
                sandwich, etc.
2. "Do you hear an /s/ or an /m/ in the middle of *emu?"*
                            hippopotamus?"
                            sausage?"
                            mustard?" etc.
3. "Do you hear an /s/ or an /m/ at the end of *moss?"*
                            comb?"
4. "Draw three horizontal lines on your chalkboard." (The teacher demonstrates this.) "I will say a word or a phrase. If you hear an /s/ or an /m/ at the beginning, write an s or an m on the first line; if you hear an /s/ or an /m/ in the middle, write an s or an m on the middle line; if you hear an /s/ or an /m/ at the end, write an s or an m on the last line." (The teacher dictates *same, master, monster, superman,* etc., and *I saw a lamb, once upon a time,* etc.)

The teacher repeats all the activities suggested for s, substituting m.

Many children have trouble in hearing sounds. The authors have consistently given direction to the children asking if they *hear* /s/. We should modify this direction to ask if children *feel* /s/ if they manifest any difficulty in responding. Paradoxically perhaps, the authors find that many children only learn to hear sounds by feeling them first. To teach the feeling of consonants requires no special training. The teacher and children say a word, e.g., *soap,* and discuss the physical placement of lips, teeth, tongue, and throat as they begin, isolating *s-s-s* if necessary. In developing this, a mirror or individual small mirrors are mandatory.

The first phoneme taught will take the longest time to teach, and it will be the hardest for most children to learn. In learning /s/ (or whatever sound is taught first), the children must learn to distinguish this from all other phonemes. In finding the letter *s* in print, children must learn to distinguish *s* from all other letters, so that much incidental learning takes place, making the subsequent learning of letters and phonemes easier. In fact, many pupils, in learning the first six to fourteen letters and sounds, discover that they know all the rest. This incidental learning does not readily take place, however, unless the first letters and phonemes are taught thoroughly.

The procedure for teaching the remaining consonants is essentially the same as for *s* and *m*.

The phoneme /r/ poses two problems. The rolled /r/ sound is preceded by a /d/: /d/r/r/r/ and may be found in the speech of German-American, Scottish-American, and Spanish-American children. Words such as *ran, ring, rat, roll, raccoon,* and *rascal* have a pure /r/ sound in the initial position. The rolled /r/ sound is used in English for the double *rr* in *burro*, but not in *burrow* or *wheelbarrow*. Spanish-American children may have difficulty in separating these sounds. *Burro* is, of course, a Spanish word, and may or may not retain its double /r/r/ roll depending on what linguistic area of the country is involved. Those areas in the Southwest that have a high percentage of Spanish-speaking citizens may accept the rolled /r/ more easily than other areas.

Asian children may have some difficulty even pronouncing /r/. They may say /l/ and therefore encode it as *l*. This can usually be corrected by having them observe the formation of the sound by a teacher or by classmates, using a mirror to watch their own imitation of the sound. They should also feel the sound as produced by touching the throat and face of someone who is pronouncing /r/. Alliterative jingles that are easily remembered are extremely useful for correcting and practicing sound distinctions.

Children enjoy making their own nonsense and sense phrases and sentences, illustrating them, and repeating them aloud to classmates. Some will develop quite complicated tongue-twisters spontaneously.

The phoneme /b/ is technically known as a *labial*, being made with the lips. Some children may not distinguish easily between /b/ and /p/ sounds, since these are both labials. This confusion may be carried over into the writing of the two letters, since they vary only slightly. For this reason, only one of these letters should be taught at a time, and the other letter should not be introduced until the first is thoroughly integrated into the children's communication. They should be able to write and read *b* as well as hear and speak /b/ before *p* is introduced at all. This principle also holds for the teaching of *m* and *n*, *d* and *t*, soft *g* and *j*, *i* and *y*, *k* and hard *c* and *q*, *s* and *z* and soft *c*, and *u* and *w*. One progression that allows the appropriate time to elapse before introducing fine distinctions in letters or phonemes is:

s	m	r	b	c (hard, as in *cat*)	t
ă (short)					
g	n	l	p	k	d
ŏ (short)					
j	f	w	v	q	
ĕ (short)					
x	z				
ŭ (short)					
ĭ (short)					

Then variations in the sounds of the vowels can be introduced, and variations in the sounds created by combining various consonants. This order should be viewed as very flexible; allowance should be made for the individual readiness of the children and for their linguistic backgrounds. The order given here is simply one rough sketch of a plan to avoid unnecessary confusion between similar phonemes and between similar letters.

The sounds of /b/ and /v/ are also confused by children of Spanish-American descent. The sounds are similar even in American-English, and for this reason /v/ should be introduced only after /b/ is mastered. During this time, a child who decodes *b* as /v/ should not be singled out for heavy correction. The teacher should be aware of the student's linguistic background and should help correct the decoding gradually. Watching and feeling the sound as it is formed in the mouth is very important, as is the practice of the sound as the class generates alliterative jingles: *Busy bees bumble beneath beautiful butterflies, bim-bam-bom booms the big bell.*

Hard /c/ as in *cat* may initially be given for words such as *kick* or *quick*, resulting in spellings like *cic* or *cwic*. Such spellings can be accepted until the letters *k* and *q* are introduced. As more and more letters of the alphabet are introduced, the children pick up the correct spellings naturally, and substitute *k* for the hard /c/ they may have been making do with. Their continued exposure to correct spelling in the form of words in books and in the words the teacher writes is their source of correction; when they are really involved in the process of communication, and really motivated to communicate, they try very hard to communicate correctly, eliminating the need for extensive correction by the teacher.

Exercises concentrating on the graphic form of letters with similar phonemes are very helpful. The children learn how to make the letters distinct when they use the form of a letter, such as *c*, in a creative illustration. The teacher can elicit discussion about what a *c* looks like--a new moon, part of a circle, a horseshoe--and then ask the children to draw pictures using the *c* as a major part. (*See the illustrations of this type of exercise on pages 53-56.*)

The sound /t/ is a dental sound, made with the teeth, as is /d/. This is why the authors separate the teaching of the two letters. Some children will decode /ð/ (the sound of *th* in *those*) as *d*; they may come from a French-Canadian background. This decoding should be accepted until the whole alphabet is taught and the teacher is in a position to begin teaching variations of sound and letter form and the combinations of consonants such as *th* as in *thin* and *th* as in *those*.

The authors recommend teaching a vowel after four to six consonants have been taught. The short vowel /ă/ seems the most practical one to begin with.

1. "The name of this letter is *a*."
2. "This letter stands for the sound of /ă/ as in *apple, ant,* and *add*."
3. "We make the sound of /ă/ with our mouths open."
4. "We write *a* like this." (Write another *a* on the chalkboard, but without any diacritical marking. At this stage, *a* represents only the sound of short /ă/.)

Isolate the vowel sound and make it distinctly. Brainstorm for words with short /ă/ sounds and observe the frequency with which this is a beginning, medial, or ending sound.

Have the children say *a* and then *at*. Have the children write *a* on their chalkboards. Ask, "What do you hear at the beginning of *at*? Write what you hear at the beginning of *at*. What do you hear at the end of *at*?" It may take four or five days to reach this point.

The teacher is now ready to teach spelling using words such as *am, bat, cat, cab, ram, sat, mat, bats, mats, tab,* etc.

Teaching the first ten spelling words will take several more days. As the teacher dictates, the children identify the number of sounds in each word. The children may put two, three, or four short horizontal lines on their chalkboards, one for each phoneme. At this stage, some children will be able to hear only some of the sounds, and even those who hear all of the sounds will not always hear them in proper sequence.

The teacher must respond to what is correct and allow for differences. The teacher should probably plan to drill all of the children each day in spelling. Much of this should be done in small groups. Of course, the teacher encourages the children in their writing to spell as they hear, so that each child drills himself many times each day as he expresses himself in writing.

Chapter IV

DEVELOPING INDEPENDENT AUTHORSHIP

In the RIOTT program, units of thought and phonics are part of each day. Children record their thoughts daily. Initially they record their thoughts through art, but *as soon as possible* they write independently *as much as possible.* Byron's work during the first week of school (*Chapter Three, pp. 94-95*) indicates what can occur when children accept this expectation. In this chapter, there are numerous examples of what can be attained after three weeks of instruction in the first grade.

Children must have drill in writing every day. As they learn phonics, they learn to write and as they learn to write, they learn phonics. Writing is practicing phonics or phonics drill, as SSR is reading drill. A major problem in initiating writing is that often the teacher presumes that young children cannot write independently. For this reason, the teacher helps too much--helps the children to copy, rather than expecting and demanding independent encoding.

The thinking comes first. The teacher motivates and provokes discussion. The writing or recording flows naturally from such discussion.

The teacher emphasizes authorship and conveys an admiration for authorship. After reading a book orally, the teacher says, "Isn't it wonderful that Mr. McCloskey put down his thoughts on pages so we could enjoy them? Wouldn't it be sad if he had never learned how to record his thoughts?"

After a stimulating discussion with the class, the teacher says, "We have had so many wonderful ideas today. We've said them all, and now they are floating away. We should save our best ideas. We should write them down. We all can be authors. We can all record our best ideas."

The teacher uses "very-own-words," basic words for writing, frame sentences, journals or diaries, etc., each day. Words and writing become part of the class environment.

1.   Very-own-words.

Sylvia Ashton-Warner, in her books *Spinster* and *Teacher* (New York: Simon & Schuster, 1959 and 1963 respectively), has written in detail about key words and their power in beginning reading and writing. She stresses that a child's very first words for writing and reading must be words that are part of the child's inner life--words that are already powerfully important to the child. Ashton-Warner writes beautifully and dynamically about key words in teaching Maori children to learn English.

A true key word is one that is learned in its first teaching and retained thereafter. Sometimes the teacher must listen closely as a child speaks, to select a potential key word. Other children can tell what key word they want when the teacher asks.

Sawicki and others have described a key-word approach with primary children in Arizona.[4] The authors of RIOTT have used, and they recommend, a form of key words that they call "very-own-words." This label seems more personal and more descriptive of the concept that children should grasp. There are ideas in a child's mind that are labeled by words; there are concepts about which he wants to talk, think, and learn more. These concepts can be fixed by one or more words, and the child can write his "very-own-words" to clarify his thinking, to retain his ideas for review, and to share his ideas with others.

Although many teachers successfully utilize the very-own-word technique by working individually with one child at a time, sometimes secretly, the authors prefer a small-group approach to the teaching of very-own-words. This approach permits stimulation of the very shy or less responsive child by the other children. It permits discussion so that concepts can be developed, again with children teaching each other. It permits many children to learn many words other than their very-own-words. It also permits the teaching and review of phonic skills.

Ten children, heterogeneously grouped so that there is ignition within the group, gather around the teacher and the chalkboard. The teacher develops (through questioning, listening, or telling) that there are hundreds and hundreds and hundreds of wonderful words in the world.

"We can choose from these hundreds of words one word for our very own, one special word. Think very hard and choose one very special word to be your very own."

John chooses *catcher's mitt*. The teacher asks why and discusses, first with John and then with other children in the group, what a catcher's mitt is, how it makes you feel to use one, how it smells, what it is made of, etc. The teacher writes the name *John* on the chalkboard in one column and *catcher's mitt* in a second column. The teacher then indicates orally that *catcher's mitt* is two words. If any phonetic elements of *catcher's mitt* have been taught, the teacher reviews these orally before writing *catcher's mitt* on the chalkboard.

For example, if the children have been taught /m/ and /t/, the teacher helps the children listen for these sounds. The teacher asks the children if they hear any sound that they know in *catcher's*. The teacher then reviews the /m/ sound and the /t/ sound and asks the children if they hear these sounds in *catcher's*. Then the teacher asks about *mitt*, pushing to have the children locate the /m/ sound at the beginning and the /t/ sound at the end of the word. After the phonemes have been located orally, the teacher then writes them on the chalkboard and fills in the other letters.

May chooses *princess* as her very-own-word, and the teacher treats it in the way that *catcher's mitt* was treated, emphasizing the meaning, extending and developing the concept, and reviewing the phonemes in *princess* that the children have been taught. The process is repeated until ten names and ten very-own-words have been listed on the chalkboard. Then each child is given his very-own-word on a 3" x 8" card or on a strip of heavy paper. The child uses his very-own-word card in many ways, but one of the most profitable uses is in that of written language.

Very-own-words can be the basis for pupil-made books. These can be simply five to ten sheets of paper stapled together; or bound, unlined notebooks. The stapling or binding seems to give a permanence that provokes greater care as the child responds. The child uses a page a day, recording his very-own-words. His recording varies with his developmental level of achievement. A typical sequence of recording would be as follows:

1. The child records his very-own-word with a picture and caption only, and discusses his thoughts with teacher and classmates.

2. The child records pictorially, and dictates his thoughts to a teacher or aide who writes them down. The child "reads" his thoughts to the teacher and then "reads" them to a partner or classmates.

3. The child records pictorially and dictates as in Step 2. The teacher encourages the child to spell orally as much of the word as he can, while she writes it for him.

4. The child records pictorially and the teacher sits with him as he writes, helping him with the spelling.

5. The child is independent except for concept development in choosing words. Many second graders and above need only Step 5.

These individual books can serve as beginning readers. Children should be allowed to teach their stories to classmates and to be taught by classmates. The books may also be taken home and read and reread to families.

The following examples are from a first-grade class during the third week of school in September. (The teacher had used some very-own-words, had begun phonics, and had taught *I* and *like* as part of a theme on animals.)

> The very-own-word *duck* comes from the unit theme, but the next page from this journal has the very-own-word *money*, which comes from the child.

> Note that in many of the journals the child's writing ability seems to far exceed his drawing ability.

money
The boy is going
to get some candy

D Whale is coming
OUT OF THE see

gorilld ı
I ⌐L IK TO GO TO
THE ZOO And I LIK TO
See THE GOnilld

Some children have difficulty in getting just their very-own-word written, but they are able to participate in the class activity.

The following is a composite of Lisa's work for the week. Her drawings for each day were colorful and expressively mature.

On Monday Lisa wrote only her very-own-word, and her teacher printed *I like trailers because they are nice.*

On Tuesday Lisa used her very-own-word *train* and left a space for *because*, which her teacher filled in.

I LIK trdins **because**
they go fast.

On Wednesday and Thursday, Lisa used her very-own-words to write short sentences.

I LiK berrys
ILiK THis dress

On Friday we see something of fruition as Lisa wrote a long sentence and wrote the word *because* by herself.

towel
ILike towel BeCause
you CaN dRYOURself

The printed word *cow* was all Tom produced on one day. It was accepted as a full day's work.

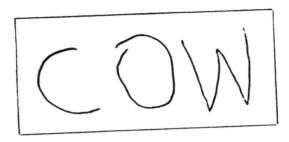

The following two days, Tom's production increased, as he both drew and wrote about *kitty* and *house*.

Kim illustrated the kind of rapid development that can be observed when children realize they can write. On successive days, Kim used the very-own-words *cow, lion,* and *squirrel.* She illustrated each animal.

On Monday she wrote only *cow,* and the teacher wrote from diction, "My cow is all colors and my mom wants to go see it."

On Tuesday Kim copied some of the words from Monday. The first line was copied from the teacher's printing and the second line from her own work.

On Wednesday Kim grew tired of copying and moved on to free expression. This movement can be directly attributed to the expectation and to the oral input from the teacher and the class, as they shared the daily results and as the children were prodded to improve the next day. (The prodding was indirect, as the teacher responded favorably and as the children responded favorably to the more mature and more individualistic expressions.)

For more skilled first-grade children, the story is a full sentence independently encoded and illustrated. For the second grade and above, the story is a paragraph or more written independently.

Stories are shared in twos and threes and shared with the whole class when everyone is finished. There is very little emphasis upon oral reading in the RIOTT approach, but in cumulative sharing oral reading is appropriate.

Very-own-words are used regularly during phonics drills, as the children hold up very-own-words in response to questions such as the following:

"Who has a very-own-word that is very big?"
        bigger than *cat*?"
        bigger than *cauliflower*?"
"Who has a very-own-word that begins like *baboon*?"
        ends like *boom*?"
        has an *m* in it?"
"Who has a very-own-word with as many syllables as
        cat?"
        cabin?"
        cauliflower?"
        hippopotamus?"
"Write on your chalkboard a very-own-word that
        has an /s/ sound in it."
        might be red."
        could be eaten."
        makes you feel scared."

2. Basic words and frames.

There are basic words that are used over and over again in all writing. Many of these words convey little meaning in isolation, and many are phonetically irregular in their spellings: *the, was, some, are, they, you, is*, etc. Such words can be taught rather easily through writing if the basic words are surrounded by words of high potency--words that are rich in meaning, such as very-own-words--provided the words are written in the natural oral language of the child.

For example, the word *is* is learned very quickly following development of the thought "happiness" or the thought "red." The children write and share pictures and sentences such as:

"Happiness is a postcard just for me."

   going out on a Saturday night."

   riding elephants."

   a new bike."

"Red is a shiny apple."

   a fire engine."

   the sun getting over the ocean."

   Martha's hair."

The word *I* is learned quickly in developing the theme **Myself.** Children talk about what they can do and illustrate what they can do. They can begin the caption (or legend) for their pictures by writing *I*. The teacher circulates and completes each caption (or legend) from the child's dictation. As individual papers are shared and as class books are made, the word *I* is learned for both writing and reading.

Frames are sometimes sentences, sometimes idioms, sometimes colorful phrases, and sometimes story patterns or poem patterns. The simplest frame might be just the word *I* followed by a balloon. The balloon is the frame.

On this work sheet, the child is expected to draw something that he can do. On the last item, he is expected to write *I* as well as draw. He is encouraged to turn the paper over and make additional frames. This exercise would follow extensive oral work--thirty to forty-five minutes spent in developing ideas about what *I* can do.

Class discussion will lead naturally to the development of two-word frames, such as the following:

"I like
"I play
"I have
"I can

The introduction to the single frame *I like* should take forty-five minutes or more of oral work. The follow-up activities and work sheets practicing *I like* should take three or more days, with culminating discussion.

Each of the frames should be introduced separately. Since the purpose of frames is to get children started if they are unable to start themselves, it is unlikely that a child would ever be expected to work on a sheet with four different frames. He is expected to be independent of the need for frames by the time he is ready for such an exercise.

For each frame, a culminating frame sheet may be used, such as the following:

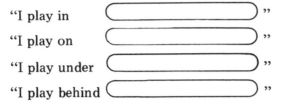

"I play in

"I play on

"I play under

"I play behind

Beginner frames can become stultifying and lead to rigid, unimaginative expression; yet many children seem to need help in getting started. The teacher must balance judiciously the demand for frames and the demand for free expression as stimulated through units of thought. Children must be encouraged to write phonetically to say what they *want* to say in the way they want to say it.

At more advanced stages, the children may work with frames such as the following:

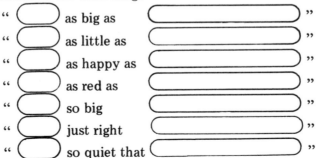

"   as big as

"   as little as

"   as happy as

"   as red as

"   so big

"   just right

"   so quiet that

The teacher will need to spend considerable time in developing frames such as these, but they can be used to encourage more colorful expression. The use of these frames will be more effective if the teacher has one or more examples from children's books. Frames taken from a book that the teacher is reading to the class are especially effective.

As the children become more sensitive to the language used by authors, they may begin to suggest interesting frames from books that they read silently. This sensitivity develops slowly, however, and it takes a great deal of oral input in its initial stages.

Sterling North's *Rascal* has been used in a seventh-grade class to develop pupils' sensitivity to descriptive language. The teacher noted with the pupils North's descriptive pattern:

> "the whirr of distant lawnmowers"
> "the singing of cicadas"
> "the clip-clop of the horses' hoofs"
> "the orchestration of the birds"
> "the first faint rattle of the coaster wagon."

The class discussed these and noted the pattern:

> "the _____ of the _____."

The pupils discussed places where they might be conscious of sounds and produced the following examples:

an airport	a classroom
a car trip	a hospital
a farmyard	a boat
a school hall	different rooms in a house
a beach	the band room
a department store	the choir room
an escalator	a car race
an elevator	

The pupils gave many examples orally, and then they wrote. They wrote about the sounds they might hear in the above places, but they added the school cafeteria, the desert, and the forest of their own volition. Such adding is common once the pupils' thinking and imagination have been sufficiently stimulated.

The pupils wrote about the farmyard:

> "the hissing of milk hitting the pail"
> "the thunder of horses running"
> "the choir of fowl in the barnyard."

The pupils wrote about the cafeteria:
   "the blurp of milkshakes"
   "the splat of a banana peel"
   "the whirr-clunk, whirr-clunk of the apple machine"
   "the thud of someone kicking the apple machine"
   "the crunch of kids munching."
The pupils wrote about the forest:
   "the little thump of the almost silent rabbit"
   "the warning splash of a beaver"
   "the creaking of pines as they rub together"
   "the whine of a chain saw"
   "the barking of a dog in the distance."
These examples and many other phrases that the pupils produced indicated that they were developing sensitivity to language, and the teacher developed this further by using passages from *True Grit* by Charles Portis. The class discussed how the following paragraphs described the season and the weather.

When I awoke there were snowflakes on my eyes.
Big moist flakes sifting down through the trees.
There was a light covering of white on the ground.

Sunrise was only a pale glow of yellow through the overcast, but such as it was, it found us mounted and moving once again. The snow came thicker and the flakes grew bigger, as big as goose feathers, and they were not falling down like rain, but rather flying dead level into our faces.[5]

The members of the class discussed the imagery; they discussed the senses used, or appealed to, in the description. The pupils were asked to think about a season or the weather and to use their "five senses," if possible, to develop a scene. They discussed the possibilities and many possible examples. The following are samples of what the class wrote:

Autumn is the crisp, cold wind blowing around your legs, the soft padding of leaves beneath your feet, and the smell of pine trees after an autumn rain. It is the beautiful yellows and oranges of the leaves and plants. It is the rustle of birds' wings as they migrate south, and it's the smell of moth balls when you take your winter clothes out of the attic. It's the feeling that winter is just around the corner.

During spring weather you can see the small children playing in the big fields. You can feel the soft, smooth grass beneath your bare feet and smell the faint sweet odor of wild flowers, not quite in full bloom. You can taste wild berries, still green. And as night falls you can hear the rhythmic chirp of crickets.

The storm all happened so suddenly. It was just-- there. We were all startled by the crashing of the thunder. It almost seemed as if the heavens had split open when a bright flash of lightning illuminated the sky. The rain sounded as if it had been held back for days and then allowed to escape. As we ran out to get the clothes that had been drying on the line, we got completely drenched. We were glad there was a storm because now the once polluted air was spring-time fresh.

Children in the primary grades and middle grades cannot be expected to produce writing of the above level, of course, but story frames can be used very early in a child's education to start him writing in an organized way. To do this, the teacher may use a set of frames such as the following:

Line One	(Name an animal.)
Line Two	(Tell what it looks like.)
Line Three	(Tell what it can do.)
Line Four	(Tell what it can't do.)
Line Five	(Say something else about it.)

Poem frames can also be used to stimulate children's thinking and feeling:

toads	_____		(animal)	_____
lions	_____		(animal)	_____
goats	_____	or	(animal)	_____
cats	_____		(animal)	_____

Poems should emphasize sense and sound, not just rhyme. All frames take lots of discussion and several examples from the class before the pupils begin individual work.

The way to prevent children from nonthinking repetition or copying is to fill the air with so many ideas about happiness, or red, or what your eyes can do, or toads, lions, goats, and cats, etc., that every child is stimulated to think and create individually distinctive work. When the air of a classroom has been enriched by one hundred to two hundred ideas about what a hole is, or what misery is, it is highly unlikely that any two children will create identical work.

All of the writing is done in an environment in which children read books and discuss books--in an environment that includes phonics instruction--in an environment that honors discussion and provokes thinking. Vernon Hale expressed this beautifully: ". . .where a skilled teacher creates an environment delicious to the senses . . . ."[6] One first-grade boy, reflecting about just such a classroom, wrote, "I go to school. It's sort of being trapped in a werl pool of thoughts."

3. Journals or diaries.

Journals are books for recording thoughts. They may be as simple as four pages stapled together with a cover; they may be notebooks of thirty-two or sixty-four pages; they may be elaborately bound volumes.

The authors have found that, in keeping a journal, children respond with greater thought and care if the journal has the permanence of a binding. Also, it is desirable to require each child to fill one page in his journal each day, in order to ensure a minimum drill in writing each day.

A journal may be used as a diary without restrictions as to entries. A journal may be a reading journal in which each child is expected to record what he reads and respond to what he has read. A journal may be a kind of assignment book in which responses to units of thought are recorded, or in which very-own-words are practiced and used in composition. A journal may be a creative writing book in which stories and poems are recorded. A journal may be for phonics, spelling, math, or social science. A journal may be a class book entitled "Our Wonderful Thoughts" or "Our Best Ideas"--a book in which children paste or make copies of work particularly enjoyed by the entire class during sharing time. Whatever a journal is, it is a cache of ideas.

Children share each other's journals, and through this sharing they teach each other much about written communication. A journal that cannot be read by classmates is not written well enough to be accepted. This is the only rule for writing.

Spelling is not corrected simply because it is not conventional. Spelling is taught (See *Spelling Through Phonics* by Marlene J. McCracken, Peguis Publishers Ltd. Winnipeg, Manitoba, 1984) and it is nagged to be as correct as the child has learned. Thus 'ft' is an acceptable spelling of 'fat' and 'btfl' is acceptable for 'beautiful' if no vowels have been taught. However, once the notion that each syllable contains a vowel sound is learned, then each syllable will be expected to have a vowel letter in it. Thus, later in grade one, 'fat' will be 'fat' and 'beautiful' will be 'butiful' or perhaps 'byoutiful' as one child spelled it. Spelling is a developmental skill and reflects both the teaching and the nagging. Nagging is correcting while the child is still writing, usually by merely pointing to the word and commenting in a way that reminds the child what he is learning. "You left the vowel out of 'fat'," or "You left out the 'a'." A good standard of handwriting and spelling are nagged so that a high quality evolves naturally.

The teacher reacts to each entry. As regularly as possible, the teacher writes a response to each child's entry. The teacher's responses are based upon the content, not upon the skills. The teacher's responses to content are communication, and such communication encourages further thinking and communication. (The teacher should, of course, observe encoding skills, punctuation, spelling, and handwriting to determine what has been taught and what needs to be taught.)

Each child should get a written response to at least every third entry. Responses should be open and honest. Responses should also be specific. If there is something wrong with the content of an entry, the teacher should indicate *what* is wrong. Otherwise, the child will be discouraged and feel frustrated.

The teacher's responding is individualized teaching at its best. Responding takes time, but it is more than worth the effort. The children get invaluable training in writing, and the teacher learns to know each child through a truly personal form of communicating.

Beginning writing can be initiated by the use of frame sentences. A frame sentence is a standard English response to a question. For example:

What can you see? = I can see a _____ .

What can you do? = I can _____ .

What can you hear? = I can hear _____ .

What can a frog do? = A frog can _____ .

What does a pirate have? = A pirate has _____ .

The Tiger Cub Readers (see Bibliography) are simple frame sentence or language patterned books which may be used for beginning reading and as a vehicle for early patterned writing. Many teachers use frame sentences to get grade one children writing at the onset of school. Others prefer a slightly less hurried approach to writing, working with less stilted attempts at written expression while continuing the kindergarten emphasis of filling children with the sounds and forms of literature, songs, and poetry.

The following four examples are typical good grade one work in September.

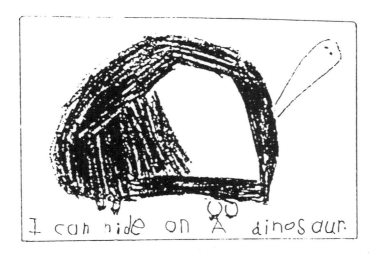

I can Ride a Vampire

I can ride on a cat

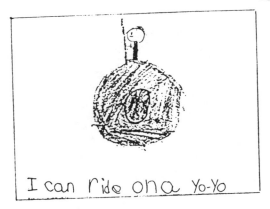

I can ride on a Yo-Yo

Valerie's work is typical of an average grade one child in September. She uses a varied form of frame responses which reflects the oral work done before writing. This is two day's work.

I CAN see a house

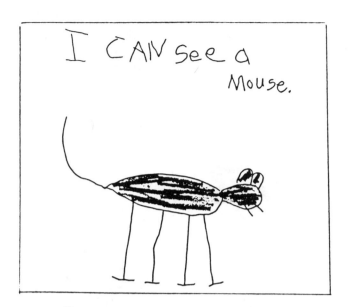

The following two examples are from a rural school with a 100% Chicano enrollment. All of the children speak Spanish at home. The kindergarten is an oral filling with language and concepts. Grade one adds spelling, journal writing and reading. We have reproduced pages from the two **poorest** journals as judged from September-November attempts.

Note that the beginning writings in October are hardly decipherable, the one December writing readable, and the January writings would be acceptable in any grade one, showing the potential of children in a whole language approach to English as a second language. The first attempts are so filled with error that a less confident teacher might have reverted to workbooks and ditto sheets.

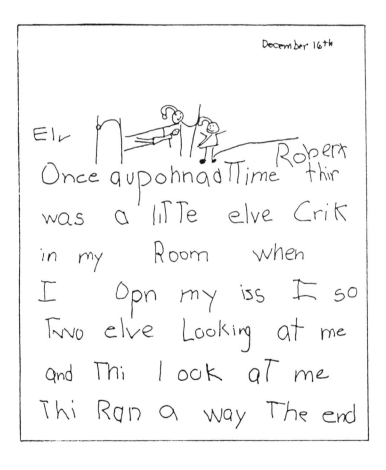

Robert

January 22nd

Once ther was a Big
Bear then He haD hieis
malph Open and I
rah a way frm the Big
Bear and I randahd He rand
of ther me and He Got me
and the Bear eat me up

and He wnt afther my
MoM and my DaD and
my DaD haD a Big
saw and my DaD trhw a
rop and then my DaD
psh the Bear Dawn my
pit Up the Big saw So
my DaD cilD the bear and
that was the end of
the Big Bear the end

Robert Jan 22nd pp 2-3

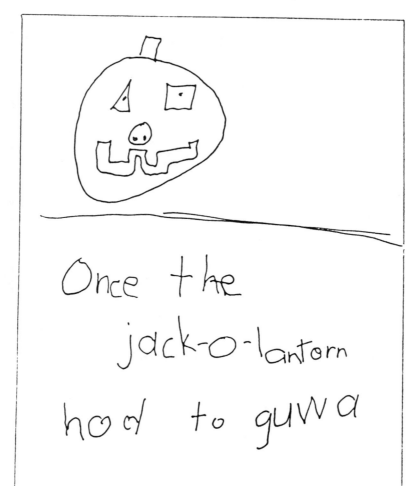

Once the
jack-o-lantorn
hod to guwa

Halloween.

Chris, October 31

Once ther was a littil
bear and it was very sad
it w as sad because it didit
have no one to care
ubat the littil bear it nod
that no boby to care ubat
that littil bear an d

chris January 22nd

it nod no body care ubat it
but then one day a littil
boy came and said hiye
said that littil boy that
littil boy said did i make you
happy said that littil boy
Saib yes it did make my happy.
  The End

Nang came to school in grade one with no kindergarten and speaking almost no English. She entered a year round school in mid July. On July 25 Nang drew a picture and labelled it apple, and dictated a sentence which the teacher recorded on the back of the picture.

One month later, Nang attempted a story.

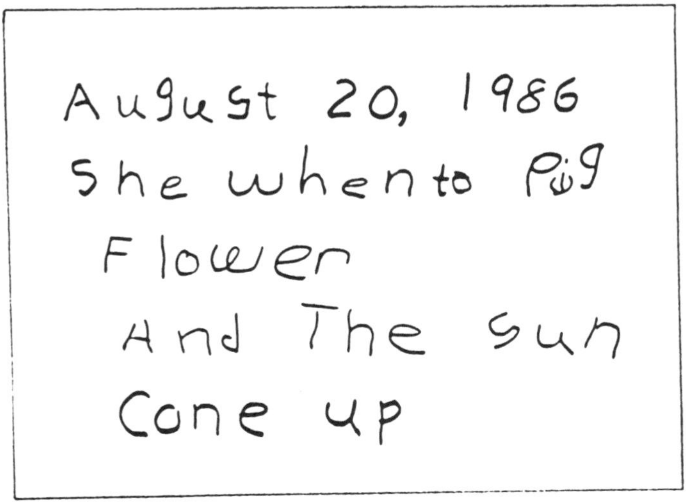

August 20, 1986
She whento Pig
Flower
And The Sun
Cone up

Two days later she wrote a second story.

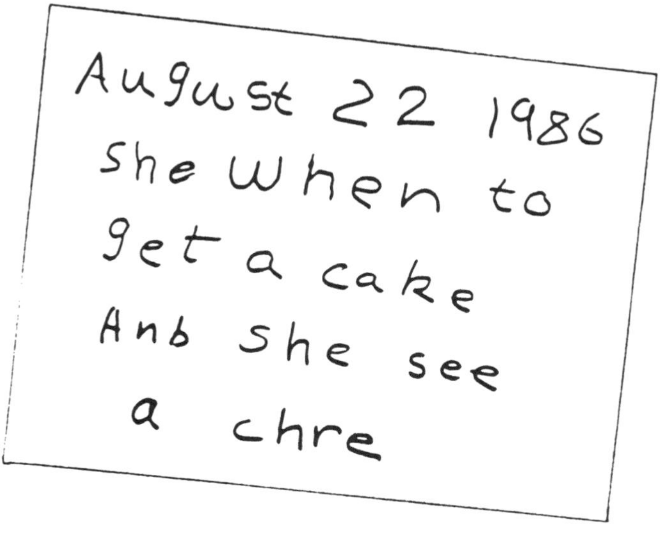

August 22 1986
She When to
get a cake
Anb she see
a chre

On September 18 Nang wrote a fairly complex story of six sentences. Nang's progress is well above average, but not unusual for children in whole language classrooms.

September 18 1986

she When to school.

And you come home.

And I Love You.

you Go When The

bus come. And I see The

rainbow. Now you Go b eb.

Susan's writing is typical for a child who came to school filled with the English language from having been read to for several years. To this the teacher added a bit of structure in the form of questions that might be answered about an animal as part of the study of animals, and there was lots of oral practice in saying stories before writing was attempted.

The word 'amphibians' was copied, but it may well be learned because the child is obviously enamored by the word and its meanings.

The following are part of an *Elephant Theme.* The children were to write a fantasy story about an elephant. The story frame was:

Once there was an elephant who had always wished to _____ . One day a _____ came and granted his wish. _____ . . .

The children spent three days, perhaps a total of two hours, creating various versions orally before writing. Three examples follow:

January 31

Once there was a sad elephant who had always wished to fly. Then one day a fairy prinsis came and granted his wish. So he could fly. he was so happy that he danst he floo to canada.

by Janet.
Grade 2

January 31.
Once there was a little
elephant who had ialways
wished to fly. Then
one day an elf came
and granted his wish.
So he was happy.
He flew to White Rock.
He had some fish and
chips and he went to
the beach.
He was very happy.
by Chris.
Grade 1

January 31
Once there was a cute
elephant who had always
wished to have a ferrari. Then
one day a green leprechaun
came and granted his wish. So
Then he got into his
ferrari and went to his
friends and he asked them if
they wanted a ride. And they
said yes. So then he gave them
a ride. The elephants thought it
was scary because it went so
fast.
by Darren
Grade 1

Another grade one class wrote using *The Longest Journey In The World* by William Barrett Morris, as a structure. They first heard the story orally, created it in the pocket chart and reread it several times. They then brainstormed for other animals and other places the animals might have travelled, and created several oral versions before writing. These writings may seem exceptional but they are not. The children have followed the story structure very closely with little variation. Many children need this kind of structure when beginning and they need lots of practice within the security of the structure before they are willing to venture into more creative expression. We must be very careful that we do not use simple structures too long before challenging children to more complex ones. The writings were done in January of grade one.

The Bee's Journey Andrea
One morning as the sun
was coming up a little
bee said to himself, "I
am going on a long journey.
He flew and he flew
and he flew. He flew
over a big flag. He flew
over the school. He flew
past the park. He flew
near the teeter-totter.
He flew by the sand.

He flew past the kids.
He flew past the slide.
He flew and he flew and he
flew. That night as the sun
was going down, the little bee
wondered How far he'd come.
So he climbed a tall tree
to look back." I am truly

amazed, " he said to himself.
This is the longest journy
in the world.

The Bunny's Journey
        by Jennifer
One morning as the
sun was coming up, a
little bunny said to
himself, "I am going on a
long journey." He hopped
and he hopped and hopped
over the bridge. He hopped
on the swings. He hopped
by the sand. He hopped
near the teeter- totters

He hopped and he hopped and he hopped. That night as the sun went down, the little bunny wondered how far he had come. So he climbed a tall pole to look back. "I am truly amazed," he said to himself. This is the longest journey in the world.

The.. Mouse's Journey, by Steven
One morning as the sun
was coming up a little Mouse
said to himself, I am going
on a long journey. He ran
and he ran and he ran.
He went by children. He
went on the sand. He went
down the slide.
He went over the bridge.
He went up the flagpole
He went on the teeter-
totters. He ran and he

and. he ran. That night
as the sun was going down,
the little Mouse wondered
how far he had run. So he
cimbed up the school
to look back. I am truly
amazed," he said to himself
This is the longest journey
in the world.

The Butterfly's Holiday.
          by   Valery.
One morning as the sun
was coming up, a little
Butterfly said to herself, "I
am going on a long
Holiday." She flew and she
flew and she flew. She flew
over the bridge. She flew
over by the slide. She
flew past the park. She
flew and she flew. That

night   as   the   sun   was
going   down,
the   little   Butterfly   wondered
how   far   she   had   come
So   she   climbed   a   tall   tree
to   look   back.   I   am   truly
amazed   she   said   to
herself.   This   is   the   longest
trip   I've   ever   had.

One way to get children to write freely is to have them rewrite a favorite story or tale. The following are grade ones' rewriting of *Goldilocks* in March. Ten children in this class wrote comparable papers.

Erica

My famuly went for a walk and they forgot the key. So a little girl named goldilocks was wandering in the woods and She saw the cotegge standing in the middle of too large trees. So She wandid over to the cotegge and she looked thrue the key hole and she did not see any body. So she looked thrue the window and she still didnot see any body So she went over to the door and opend It up, and wolkd insid The first thing she saw was my teddy bear. She pcked it up and played with it.

then she went up to my
room and she saw my pensle
croans and she picked oun
up and she skribld all over
the playce And wene I saw
that I was very angry so
I thrue her out the window!
the end.

Kelly
One day when we were
having brecfrist it was too hot
So we went to the park
until it was cool. But
wall we were there
a little girl came dong
and peaed inside. And
on the tailde she saw
three plats with eggs.
first she trid my mom's
egg. But it was too cold.
then she trid my

dad's egg but it was too hot. then she trid my egg and it was just rite. then she wan to go for a nap so she went upsters to have a nap but when she woke up she herd a noys. bang! then she went down sters to see wut was the mater but we were home. And my dad said sowebody has been eating my egg. sombody has been eating my egg said my mother. Sudenleay they saw her. And they yelld at her. And we chast her out and she never came back again.

Darren

One day my family went for a drive. well we were gone a little girl named Goldilocks came. First she peeped through the window. Next she looked in the keyhole. Then she enterd through the window. First she tried my dad's telephone but it was too heavy. Then she tried my moms telephone but it was too soft. Then She tried my telephone. It was just night. Then she went and tried on some shoes. First she tried my dad's shoes. They were too big. Then she tried my mom's shoes. They were too small. Then she tried my shoes. They were just right. Then she went upstairs and tried my dad's bed. it was too big. Then when we came home and saw her she saw us and scamprd out of the house.

Mandy, in a different grade one, wrote as follows when her class all rewrote *The Gingerbread Boy.* She began on March 7th. Everyone else in the class wrote two or three pages.

Mandy   March 7

There was an old woman and an old man. The old woman made a gingerbread boy. the gingerbread boy ran away from the Little old woman and the little old man. The woman and the man said "stop stop," but the gingerbread boy kept on running. Then the gingerbread boy met a dog. The dog said "stop stop" I want to see you." "No" said, the gingerbread boy. The ginger bread boy kept on running

Mandy   March 7

Then the ginger bread boy met a goat. The goat said "stop stop" but the ginger bread boy kept on running. Then the ginger bread boy met a fox. The fox said "stop stop" but the ginger bread boy kept on running. Then the ginger bread boy met a cat. The cat said "stop stop" but the ginger bread boy kept on running. Then the ginger bread boy met a rabbit. The rabbit said "stop stop" but the ginger bread boy kept on running.

The story continued for three more pages on March 7 and then for five pages on March 8, when her teacher said, "Mandy, one of the hardest things to do when writing is to know how to stop." Reluctantly Mandy wrote:

Mandy   March 8

Then the ginger bread boy met Jody Jody said "stop stop" but the ginger bread boy kept on running. Then the ginger bread boy met Joanne.

Joanne ate the ginger bread boy. The old woman was sad because Joanne ate him.

4. Achievement.

Most of the examples of pupils' work are the work of boys. Boys' work was chosen not because it is better than girls' work, but because many teachers feel that boys are not as responsive to language as girls are, and because many studies indicate that boys perform poorly in language, compared to girls.

The authors have found little observable difference in the achievement of boys and girls when children are taught with the RIOTT program. Many teachers who have tried the program have expressed surprise that the boys did so well.

The RIOTT program does not, of course, eliminate individual differences in achievement. Instead, it accentuates and capitalizes upon these differences.

It does, however, eliminate the nonreader-nonperformer, and the disproportionately high percentage of girls among the top achievers (although this program does not group children in the traditional sense). The girls continue to achieve well, and the boys match the girls' high achievement.

With pupils of both sexes, a factor of paramount importance is the teacher's *faith*--faith that the RIOTT program will open new doors of learning for the children. The authors' faith in this program has been reaffirmed many times by what the children themselves have written. The authors will always treasure what a fourth-grade boy named Larry wrote:

MY SCHOOL

School is the place where you spend most of your life.

You worry about it when you are not there, for you know you're getting older every minute. Then, when you do get there there's something going on all the time, and you forget about the worry for you are so busy.

Then it is time to go home, when you haven't even had enough of that one day.

So you look forward to to-morrow, hoping they'll open the doors at 8 A.M. so you can get a good early start on living.

In submitting a copy of Larry's story, his teacher wrote: "This experimental plan is a tremendous amount of work for the teachers, but when you read such an article from such a young student, you feel somehow that the effort is well worth it."

Chapter V

SILENT READING *and* DISCUSSION

The reading program in every school should develop each child's ability to read silently and to sustain himself when reading silently without interruption for a relatively long period. As noted in Chapter One, such reading is called sustained silent reading (SSR).

1. Sustained silent reading.

SSR is a vital part of the RIOTT program, and it is something every child should do every day. SSR is the *drill* of silent reading; it is the drill or practice necessary in learning to read.

Fortunately, SSR requires no special materials or special equipment other than a timer. It requires no special teacher training or expertise.

To initiate SSR, the teacher follows six rules rigidly. After the SSR habit has been established, the teacher may vary from the rules. Usually it takes only a few days to establish SSR, but in some cases it may take very much longer. At any rate, there should be no variation from the following rules until SSR has been firmly established.

1. *Begin with the whole class.* Groups of ten or fewer children sometimes can't get started. Children in small groups tend to break the rules for SSR--to ask the teacher for help and expect a response. (Heterogeneously-grouped classes are easier to start than homogeneously-grouped classes.)

2. *Each child selects one book.* (No book-changing is permitted.) Kindergarten and first-grade children may choose a book from a pile, as suggested in Chapter One. Older children select books at the library prior to SSR time and have their books in the classroom. If a child forgets to get a book, or for some other reason does not get one, the teacher should be able to offer a wide selection from within the classroom. (No child should be chided for selecting a book that is too easy or too hard.)

3. *Each child must read silently.* He must interrupt no one. The implication of this rule is that "I, the teacher, believe and know that you can read silently, so don't pretend that you can't."

4. *The teacher reads silently.* The teacher selects something very interesting to read and remains engrossed in it until the SSR time comes to an end. The teacher must set a good example. She must permit no interruption of her reading if *all* of her pupils are to respond to the group compulsion to read.

5. *A timer is used.* An alarm clock or minute-timer (such as is used for cooking) is set and placed where no child can see its face. A wall clock does not work initially; the reluctant readers become clock watchers. Nor can the teacher act as the timer; children will interrupt to ask if time is up. Start with two to five minutes. When the timer rings, the teacher says, "Good. You sustained yourselves today. Continue reading silently if you wish." Most classes will choose to continue, and the children will maintain themselves for twenty to fifty minutes more. The teacher notes the class's sustaining power and the next day sets the timer forward so that it almost reaches the

sustained reading time of the first pupil who quit reading.

6. *There are absolutely no reports or records of any kind.* The children do not even keep a list of books they have read. Book discussions, writing, and record-keeping develop naturally later on as sustained silent reading becomes a habit. Initially, they are simply an unnecessary obstacle that encourages reluctant readers not to participate.

During the first week, the teacher follows the six rules without exception. If the children have responded as expected, they will be sustaining themselves in silent reading for thirty minutes by the end of the week. After a few weeks, when the class has practiced a sustaining span of thirty minutes, the teacher may vary somewhat from the rules. Two ten to fifteen minute periods of SSR each day may be more feasible for kindergarten and grade one. *Rules 3 and 4 remain inviolable.* Deviations from Rule 2 are comparatively rare.

The teacher ends the SSR period by reacting to the book that the teacher has read. The teacher may:

1. summarize in one sentence the main idea or theme of the book
2. read a paragraph from the book and relate it to current happenings, national events, or something in school
3. use a dictionary to check a word in the book and comment about unusual usage of the word
4. have the children ask questions about the book and develop models of questioning so that the pupils learn to go beyond simple recall-type questions
5. describe how some episodes in the book have supplied ideas about teaching or working with the pupils
6. begin to keep a journal of interesting words, phrases, ideas, etc.

Such action by the teacher sets models for the pupils to use. Through practice, and from adult example, every child should learn to read silently and to sustain himself in a book for a reasonably long time.

Every child, from kindergarten through high school, should be required to read silently, without interruption, for at least thirty minutes a day. Every young person must have enough time to teach himself how to read, and he must drill himself until he becomes proficient.

2. Discussing books.

Children need to be taught *how* to discuss books. The techniques of discussion are not greatly different from those described previously, in which the teacher read to the children from books or stimulated discussion based upon a unit of thought. Discussions stimulated by books that the children have read are really an extension of the discussion skills already developed.

The teacher must structure the discussion sessions if they are to be productive and stimulating. There should be three areas of questioning: the thinking skills of recall, interpretation, inference, etc.; personalization through empathy and feelings; and vocabulary development. The broad objectives remain the same from kindergarten through the sixth grade or the eighth grade: to develop thinking skills through reading, writing, listening, and speaking; to develop each child's ability to respond personally to the characters in a story; and to develop each child's vocabulary.

Several taxonomies have been developed to describe levels of thinking or reading skills. The authors feel that these taxonomies are useful as guides to the teacher in developing questioning skill. A simple taxonomy of three levels is adequate for most teaching purposes.

Level 1:   *Recognition and recall.*
This is reading at its simplest, locating information or an answer and recalling it.

Level 2:   *Inference, interpretation, and evaluation.*
This requires recognition and recall plus some personal input in developing meaning. This may be a hierarchy with inference preceding interpretation, and interpretation preceding evaluation.

Level 3:   *Appreciation, empathy, and application.*
This last level requires all of the first two

plus a personalization or internalization of response.

For example, if the teacher developed questions based upon *The Boy Who Never Listened*, the following questions might be asked:

Level 1:   "Why didn't Tom hear many noises?"

"What caused Tom to become quiet?"

"What noises did Tom hear after he had been to the dentist?"

Level 2:   "Why didn't Tom notice or listen to sounds when he was going to the dentist?"

"How did Tom feel as he was going home? Why did he feel that way?"

"Could a boy be so noisy that he never really heard things?"

"What does this story tell you about how you learn?"

"Could a tooth ache so much that you wouldn't hear things on the way to the dentist?"

Level 3:   "How would you feel or act if you had a toothache?"

"Would you want to listen to things? Why or why not?"

"If we went for a walk in the jungle, how should we behave?"

"Should we be noisy or quiet? When? Why?"

The teacher may feel that it is necessary to read each story to question effectively. This is necessary for Level 1 questions if they are specific. The teacher can, however, develop questions without having read the book. Such questioning utilizes the title or the main idea elicited from the pupil and goes from a broad general question to the specific. The questions grow from the child's responses. Based upon the same story title, *The Boy Who Never Listened*, the teacher might lead a discussion as follows:

"Who was the boy who never listened?"

"Why didn't he listen?"

"Did he ever learn to listen? When?"

These three questions should elicit enough information so that the teacher could now develop the questions previously listed for Level 2 and Level 3.

Thus far, the material on book discussions may imply that each child has read the same book or that all the children in the class discuss a book. Many times this is so. There should, however, be many discussion sessions in which each child has read a different book, and there should be many discussions by groups within the class so that five, ten, or fifteen children participate in a particular discussion.

Groupings for discussion should be for a definite purpose; discussion groups very rarely should be homogeneous by ability. The main reasons for groups rather than participation by the whole class are to permit more speaking time for each pupil in the group and to permit the pupil some choice about which discussions he participates in.

Once the children have been taught to discuss books, more than one group can discuss at one time. Teacher participation is not mandatory. One group may discuss, with teacher direction, while the remainder of the class works quietly on other activities, or one group might discuss while the teacher works with the rest of the class.

It is necessary for the teacher to demonstrate the format for discussions. This can be done by discussing the adult book or books that the teacher has been reading during SSR and augmenting the example from a simple children's book.

For example, suppose that the teacher has read Hannah Green's *I Never Promised You A Rose Garden.* The teacher shows the book to the children and reads the title aloud.

The teacher says, "This title is a good title because it tells one of the main ideas in the book. It does not say the main idea directly, but in a way that makes you think. What do you think the title means?"

The children respond, and the teacher accepts and develops the responses. To encourage the flow of responses, no answer should be labeled "right" or "wrong." There is no "right" answer, so ideas are encouraged to flow.

Next, the teacher says, "This book is about sanity and insanity or craziness. It tells of a young girl, Deborah, who is crazy, struggling to become sane. Deborah complains that trying to be sane is hard work. Her psychiatrist says, "I never promised you a rose garden." She is saying poetically, indirectly, that being sane is not easy. We all have times when just being a person is hard. Are there times when you find it difficult to be pleasant, times when it is hard to be yourself?"

The teacher develops the idea that a rose garden would be a place that is pleasant, peaceful, and beautiful. The teacher asks, "Is life always peaceful? Is it always pleasant?" The children discuss these ideas, and they discuss the "goodness" or "poorness" of the title.

The teacher then reads aloud *The Boy Who Never Listened* or refers to a book (or books) that have been read to the class. The teacher discusses the theme of *The Boy Who Never Listened,* and the children discuss the suitability of the title.

"Is it a good title? Why? Why not?"

"Does the title describe the whole book?"

"Does the title describe (directly or by metaphor) the theme of the book?"

At this point, several groupings are possible. The children are invited to consider the book that they have just finished in SSR and to join a group to present, discuss, and justify:

1. their book's title as a good title to suggest the main idea of the book
2. their book's title as a misleading title to suggest the main idea of the book
3. their book's title as a direct statement or a metaphor (Is the book's title more like *I Never Promised You A Rose Garden* or more like *The Boy Who Never Listened*?)

The teacher will need to present examples several times in developing different kinds of discussion responses to a book. Many types of discussion should be developed. Discussion groups can and should be formed around ideas, as for example:

1. "This book taught me something that is most unusual. It is something I never knew before or thought about much before. It tells me that I can kill an octopus very simply by biting it between the eyes. Did you find something in your book that particu-

larly interested you? Do you think it is a fact? Can you find out if it really is a fact?"

2. "This book showed me that a person may behave in a way that I think is bad, and yet when I understand the reasons I realize I might have behaved in the same way. Bill was rich and forty years old. He wanted to help the poor people, but he thought his friends and his wife, particularly, would think he was crazy if he gave his money to the poor people or used his money to help them, so he did nothing. He did nothing until his life and his wife's life were threatened, and he used this as an excuse for helping the poor. I want to praise Bill for his generosity, but I don't like or admire him because he could not do what he wanted to for fear of offending his friends. I've probably done the same kind of thing, but I still don't admire it. Do any of the characters in your books behave in a way that bothers you? Does the author show why the character behaved badly?"

3. "This book demonstrates several ways in which animals help man survive. The author says that a single bird may eat as many as four hundred mosquitoes in one day. Do any of you have books in which animals help man?"

These three examples are condensed. When working with a class, the teacher will be more expansive, and the teacher will read excerpts from the book to illustrate personal conclusions or ideas.

Discussion groups can and should form around literary devices and examples of them *when the children are sufficiently developed* to deal with these devices. Again, the teacher should demonstrate. The following are some of the literary devices that may be used when the children are ready for them:

1. alliteration
2. metaphor
3. enjoyable repetition
4. flashback
5. mood development, etc.

Discussion groups should also be formed for vocabulary discussion of the following:

1. unusual words not seen before
2. usual words used in an unusual context
3. interesting descriptive words
4. unusual action words
5. words with several meanings in which context is necessary to determine the meaning, etc.

Discussion groups should also be formed for discussion based on empathy or feeling:

1. "I wanted to meet the main character because _____."
2. "I disliked the person because _____."
3. "This was really funny because _____."
4. "I was terribly frightened by _____ because _____." etc.

Discussion groups should, of course, be formed around the ideas in a single book that a single child presents for discussion. This will be a form of book report and book publicity, and it will grow naturally from the children's reading in SSR.

Vocabulary discussion is perhaps the most difficult to foster successfully. Vocabulary study easily disintegrates into keeping word lists of prescribed words or of a prescribed number of words. The teacher must seek ways of demonstrating a personal interest in words and an enthusiasm for the whole process of communication. Such interest and enthusiasm is, to some extent, contagious, and eventually the children will catch some of the enthusiasm.

Vocabulary can be built effectively through discussion prior to the writing activities of the children. For example, the teacher may use a single page from a story, such as page 37 from *The Boy Who Never Listened:*

"Teeny Tom heard all kinds of sounds.
He heard happy sounds. He heard sad sounds.
He heard soft sounds. He heard loud sounds."

The teacher or the children may form groups of pupils to list various kinds of sounds such as "happy sounds," "soft sounds," and "loud sounds." Each group of pupils should come up with many sounds.

The "happy sounds" may be ranked by degrees of happiness, with much discussion about which of two sounds is happier.

"Is the sound of Santa Claus whooshing down the chimney happier than the bell of Santa's reindeer?"

"Is the sound of the first robin in spring happier than the first snow of winter?"

The happy sounds may be arranged in patterns, groups, or stanzas to express joy, or they may be used as story starters for pupils to describe their happiest day.

From the group discussion, the pupils may be encouraged to find the happiest word in the book they are now reading, the happiest sentence, or the happiest paragraph. The same activity may be developed for "soft" or "loud" sounds, etc.

The teacher should keep two maxims in mind when discussing books. First, when giving examples, the teacher should discuss only those books in which the teacher has an honest interest and which the teacher finds personally stimulating. Second, the teacher must abandon the idea that questions beyond the level of recognition and recall need absolute answers.

Driving toward consensus can kill a discussion. When there is an answer (or an answer key) to the question, "What was the main idea of the poem or story?" or "What is the happiest sound?" there is a damper to discussion. A fixed answer leaves little to discuss.

Although a class may reach agreement, seeking agreement is not the objective. When agreement is reached, discussion usually ends. A teacher who wants discussion must stimulate children to think of alternatives and then help the children to evaluate the alternatives and the alternative ways of expressing ideas.

Free-flowing, enthusiastic discussion can be one of life's most pleasant and rewarding experiences. Thus the development of discussion skills should begin when a child's education begins--and should continue through the years.

3. General discussion.

Discussion related to books is only a part of the development of oral language skills. Discussion of a more general nature is also essential in building oral language skills--especially in the beginning of the program.

Throughout this guide, the authors have emphasized the importance of oral input as a motivating factor and as a generator of ideas. Oral summary, sharing, and discussion help children to clarify their thinking and help the class to feel a sense of unity.

Some teachers may presume that five to ten minutes of introductory discussion is adequate when getting children to respond to questions such as "What do you like?" "How big is big?" and "What can your feet do?" The fact is that after a discussion lasting only ten minutes, children's written or drawn responses are often repetitive and uninspired.

It is perfectly natural for a teacher to feel that the discussion should be halted when the children seem to have run out of ideas. But this is not the time to give up. It is the time to expand the discussion through the use of additional questions that involve the children personally.

Provoking children to think is sometimes difficult, but if they are encouraged to think about themselves and their reactions, they will eventually respond. Questions such as the following will evoke enough thinking and responses to make an entire class period of discussion rewarding.

What do you like?
           to eat?
                      on Sundays?
                      at school?
                      on picnics?
                      after going to the movies?
                      when you go out for lunch?
                                  for dinner?
                      after school?
                      at birthday parties?
                      that you carry in your pocket?
                          is frozen?
                        is raw?
                        must be cooked?
                        is boiled? fried? baked? etc.
                        is red? green? blue? white? etc.

comes in a can? a carton?
a bottle? a jar? etc.
with your fingers?
that you can't eat with your fingers?
tastes sweet? sour?

What do you like to do at home?
school?
the park?
on the street?
at the ocean?
in the mountains?
at your friends house?

What do you like to do at your uncle's? grandmother's? etc.
at night? three o'clock? etc.
in your kitchen? basement? etc.
on Saturdays? Mondays? etc.
with a friend? your brother? etc.
hammer? saw? tent? carton? etc.
in a car? truck? trailer? camper? boat? etc.
in summer? fall? etc.
for work?
for fun?

What do you like to see outdoors? indoors?
at home? school? the grocery store? etc.
on television?
on the dinner table?
when you look in the mirror?
your friends doing? wearing?

This list of questions could be expanded to one hundred or two hundred questions, but usually the questions shown above will provoke at least forty minutes of thinking. (This is not easy work for the teacher, but it is essential to stimulate the children to think and to express themselves orally.)

Frequently, one question will provoke a discussion for ten or more minutes; more frequently, one child's response will lead to many other responses. If the teacher reacts sensitively to the responses of the children, discussions will develop naturally and establish the atmosphere of openness and verbal freedom that motivation and learning require.

All children, except those with certain handicaps, come to school with some oral language skill. By building upon what they already have, the teacher develops the necessary base for the acquisition of writing and reading skills.

Writing and reading are basically solitary skills to be practiced alone. But oral communication--talking and listening--is chiefly a social skill, best practiced in groups. Fortunately, children of different ability levels operate together effectively in oral communication. There is no need to have ability grouping; it is, in fact, contra-indicated.

There is also another good reason for emphasizing oral language: it permits the teacher to teach more efficiently in certain situations. A group of thirty children learning together, stimulated by the teacher and inspiring each other, is more effective than three groups of ten children (or thirty children learning separately) because of the greater interreactional scope of discussion with the whole class.

There are times for individual teaching, and there are times for total-class instruction. Some teachers have been made to feel guilty about large-group instruction because of the current emphasis upon individualization. But the key to individualization is in the *responses*, not in the teaching. Teaching that demands identical responses from each child at different times does not seem to the authors to be individualized at all. It is, in fact, more lockstep than the traditional teaching it is supposed to supplant.

The heart of any truly individualized program must be in the individual character of what the child does--not in his doing his learning alone. The RIOTT program *is* individualized because it promotes individualized responses, yet it utilizes total-group and large-group teaching for much of the instructional program.

This aspect of the program should provide considerable comfort to teachers who have been assigned to large classes. They can rest assured that, for the purpose of discussion, large groups are definitely preferable to small ones.

Chapter VI

In the RIOTT program, as in any learning program, there are many factors that affect its success. Some are beyond the control of the teacher; others are within their control. We recognize that administrative non-support and pressure to teach other programs can render a teacher inept.

Accountability and testing have evolved as the locusts of the seventies and eighties. They are part of the back to basics movement. Children are skill taught and tested for no useful purpose, so much so that the goals of education in some schools have become the test scores. Kindergarten children spend their days learning the alphabet which probably was taught in nursery school, and learning their sounds. Having a two year old who knows the alphabet or a four year old who reads are status symbols. An early start and getting ahead have made learning to read into a race. Instead of developing a love of language through hearing and seeing stories, through dramatic recreation, dance and art, and developing a sense of wonder of the world about them through observation, exploration, and talking, five year old kindergarten children color and x their way through six or more workbooks to develop reading readiness skills, and are tested to see if they have learned. As far as we can determine many of these children learn two things: They learn how to take tests by practising the test format in their workbooks, and they learn that school is vapid, boring and empty.

State and Provincial legislatures too often seem committed to the notion that tests of achievement and accountability will cause teachers to teach better and cause all children to achieve above average. Their mandates do cause teachers to behave differently. Our observations lead us to believe that the differences are undesirable. Teachers focus on skills without content or communicative purpose. The absurdity of the mandate that children should all be at or above average defies mathematical reality and should be obvious. However, the misconception has been with us for years and antedates the accountability movement. It is harder to teach well in the 1980's than it was in the 1960's. There are more constrictions affecting teachers than there were twenty or thirty years ago.

1. Open Education

Open education, a hope of the sixties, is gone from the educational scene. No one talks about it in 1986. The beliefs that we thought open education were based upon are still valid, and these beliefs are inherent in the whole language approach to teaching and learning. Open education still offers a high potential for pupil success. It is a process that allows the teacher to sense challenge, overcome frustrations, and reap gratification as all children succeed in becoming literate.

Open education did not quarrel with tradition simply because it was traditional. Open teaching acknowledged individual differences in learning and response styles, but it did not and does not abandon the teacher's responsibility to teach, to direct, to set goals, to demand, to admonish, and to behave as a senior member of society.

If there is one fact standing out from the thousands of conclusions that may be drawn from educational research on reading and writing in the past fifty years, it is that **children rarely learn what is *not* taught,** and that **children rarely fail to learn what *is* taught if the teacher believes that the children are capable of learning and demands that the children practice.** This is true whether the teaching is formal or informal, open or traditional, and whether what is taught is useful or sensible. Many children do daily worksheets whose sole result is achievement test scores that "demonstrate" accountability. The essential part of open education is the freedom to think, to examine ideas, and to learn without penalty for mistakes. This creates a tenet that children's responses are never wrong and that responses are neither wrong nor right. Responses are honest attempts to learn, to think, or to practice thinking. Children learn to think by thinking, not by learning correct answers through memorization or outwitting the teachers.

To think requires the following conditions:

1. The knowledge of certain facts.
2. A perception of the facts.
3. Freedom to peruse, exam, question, and experiment with the facts without penalty or duress to conform.
4. Practice in thinking.

These four conditions are so intertwined that they cannot be separated except for presentation or discussion. They all exist together or thinking does not develop. Any fact must be perceived. New facts are related to old within the brain's storehouse or they are ignored. New facts are related to old because the brain directs the senses much more than the senses direct the brain. Thinking is classifying and reclassifying perceptions within the brain. Thinking is learned by thinking; the brain does this instinctively. The brain continues to think unless we corrupt it by our teaching and demands. Thinking is making sense out of the world by making sense out of our perceptions. It results in a memorization of sorts because we tend to remember what we understand. If we, as teachers, insist that children merely accumulate facts — by memorizing *our* "facts" as *we* understand them — we may cause them to stop thinking because they do not have our background of experiences through which to understand the facts. If the children do think, they do not agree with teacher because they do not understand. If they do not understand they cannot remember. They stop thinking and attempt to memorize the "school facts" in isolation.

Thinking may be simply joining together two perceptions that you have never joined before. If I ask, "How are elephants and skunks alike?" and you respond that both can spray, never having been taught that answer and never before having thought that answer, then whatever your brain did was thinking. Thinking may be more complex, obviously, when you join together several, possibly hundreds, of individual perceptions. We join things together because they are alike, or we cast them out because they do not belong. The brain seems to do this automatically as we

make new perceptions. Those perceptions which cannot fit any-
where seemingly are ignored. Those which can fit seem to be
stored in some network to be recalled when wanted. The brain
seems akin to a muscle; the more it is used, the more it seems to
develop tone and flexibility. The less it is used, the more it seems
to atrophy.

To classify we:
1. recall facts
2. remember details
3. organize information and ideas
4. make inferences
5. draw conclusions
6. evaluation information
7. understand words
8. Etc. (This list is illustrative, not definitive.)

These skills are found in almost every professional text on the
teaching of reading, and in every basal reader manual and workbook. They are labelled reading comprehension skills, and
perhaps they are if they occur while reading. However, anyone
writing a letter, watching a TV show, listening to a story being
read, watching a film, and so on, is just as likely to practice those
skills. We contend that these are all descriptors of thinking skills
that the brain does. We further suggest that when the brain thinks
it does not worry about the modality of input; the brain actions
are the same whether we watch a film or read a book or talk with
a friend. We add to this the notion that skills learned in meaningful situations transfer to new situations and they transfer in direct
proportion to the meaningfulness of the learning. Whole language
learning and open education both provide meaningful learning
environments so that transfer of skills is highly likely. One of the
most evident situations of meaningless learning is the inability
of children to spell on Monday the words they did perfectly on the
Friday spelling list, another is the perfect scores of remedial students on phonics worksheets without any transfer to silent reading. Conversely, we find that when we teach children to spell so
that phonics makes sense, then their daily spelling is as good as
their Friday tests.

M. Jerry Weiss at the 1977 summer reading conference at
Western Washington University said that to develop a pupil's
thinking a teacher must raise questions while abandoning the an-

swer key or the notion of single right answers. This is not to deny the importance of facts, but it suggests that the teacher's role is to supply the facts as they fit particular situations and then require children to work with them.

"Right answers" require that we pay attention to some facts and ignore some others. Right answers require that we have some particular bits of information and that we ignore or don't have others. As a very simple example, a grade one reading workbook in the 1940's had the statement "Children are in school all the time." The answer key said "No." One child circled "Yes" explaining that the earth revolved so that while he was out of school children on the other side of the world were in school, and that when it was summer in his northern part of the world it was winter in the southern. Obviously he knew too much and had not yet learned to ignore what he wasn't supposed to know. *The facts that we know affect what we think.*

The way in which we perceive the facts also affects our thinking. If we are trained to look for certain things we tend to see them while an untrained person will ignore them. Every profession trains its neophytes to attend to certain facts or behaviors. It is not the issue here to argue whether the facts are correct but to argue that our perception is always biased (sometimes prejudiced) by our training and our experiences. If we have been bitten once, or several times, by a German shepherd dog we are likely to regard all dogs warily and to think of German shepherds as vicious. If we are blind and have a German shepherd as a guide dog we are very unlikely to consider any German shepherds as vicious. The brain's storehouse determines how we perceive new or repeated experiences. We tend to observe in terms of our stored experiences so that a change of perception is difficult; we want to see things the way we expect to see them because 'impolite' facts cause us mental distress, so much so that we are likely to distort and misperceive particularly impolite facts rather than see the true facts. (Of course, the true facts are merely someone else's perception of certain facts.)

Jeanne Chall gives us an example of this in *Learning to Read, The Great Debate*

> ". . . Several times when I thought I had detected extreme apathy and listlessness in a group of bored children, the author of the reading program or an enthusiastic supervisor sitting beside me exclaimed: 'Isn't it wonderful how

the children are enjoying it!' Personal investment in a particular reading program can destroy perspective and make one see what one wants to see rather than what is actually there." (p. 269)

(Obviously, this whole section on thinking and perception is one person's perception and is liable to the same distortion.)

D. L. Rosenhan ("On Being Sane in Insane Places," **Science, 179:250-258, January 19, 1973.**) discusses the role of perception in what is seen or heard. He was concerned with whether we, the sane, could judge accurately who is insane, and he discusses our inability to tolerate not knowing. He devised an experiment in which eight normal, productive adults sought self admission to mental hospitals, with four seeking a second self admission. All were promptly admitted, diagnosed as insane (eleven schizophrenic and one a manic-depressive). No psuedopatient ever seemed to have been suspected of sham by any hospital employee although they all responded as normally as possible. They were discharged in 7 to 52 days with their insanity in remission. All of the psuedopatients were questioned by the other inmates who recognised them as fakes, so that the study does not question if insanity exists; it questions our ability to diagnose it and examines the role of expectation in distorting our perceptions. It tests the hypothesis that "psychiatric diagnoses are in the minds of the observer and not valid summaries of the characteristics displayed by the observed." (p. 235)

One hospital superintendent learned that Rosenhan had sent a psuedopatient and challenged Rosenhan to send another, saying that his staff would identify the psuedopatient. Rosenhan agreed to send one or two within a thirty day period. Rosenhan sent no one. The hospital staff identified roughly one half the 90-plus patients admitted during that period as suspect, affirming Rosenhan's contention that we see what we are trained to see or what we expect to see.

Rosenhan discusses the human need to know, the unwillingness of the brain to be able to accept ambiguity. He states: "Whenever the ratio of what is known to what needs to be known approaches zero, we tend to *invent* 'knowledge' and assume that we understand more than we actually do. We seem unable to acknowledge that we simply don't know. The need for diagnosis and remediation of behaviorial and emotional problems is enormous.

But rather than acknowledge that we are just embarking on understanding, we continue to label patients as 'schizophrenic', 'manic-depressive', and 'insane', as if in those words we have captured the essense of understanding. The facts of the matter are that we have known for a long time that diagnoses are often not useful or reliable, but we have nevertheless continued to use them. We now know that we cannot distinguish insanity from sanity. It is depressing to consider how that information will be used." (p. 257)

We interpret the Rosenhan study to support two notions: (1) Perception is primarily controlled by the brain directing the senses rather than the senses directing the brain. Thus, if we want to create different thoughts or thinking we must be very much concerned with the mind set prior to the presentation of information, and, within ourselves, we must be very much aware that our own beliefs prejudice our presentation. (2) The brain may not like to think differently. It is born to respond to stimuli and it must make sense of those stimuli before it can stop responding. The brain seeks rest even though it is built to respond. This is the paradox of the brain. It does not like to think differently; it is more likely to misperceive than to puzzle about impolite facts or perception. The brain seeks rest, not correctness, and yet the brain functions by not being at rest. This is a dilemma for teachers. Awareness of this brain functioning dictates that teaching is more than accumulating facts or the correct interpretation of facts. No child ever gives wrong answers to questions. His answers are always right in that they are the sum total of what he knows as he has perceived it and they reflect the amount of practice he has had in thinking.

It seems unlikely that thinking can be taught by an emphasis upon "right answers". These right answers may be secured *without* thinking as many school children have learned. Right answers require conformity of experiences and perception, so much so that right answers may require an unreal degree of sameness. Any adult has had too many years of experience to make an answer key for children. Their "right answers" may require children to memorize nonsense because agreeing with the answer would force them to reject the sum total of their experiences or their intuition which senses something as wrong. This learning of *wrong* answers denies ones' own self, a process destructive to the human being, and one which most of us find intolerable.

2. The theme approach to learning.

A theme approach to learning is one of the best ways to achieve an educationally open classroom. A theme differs from a work unit. In a standard work-unit approach to learning, the teacher collects all the necessary materials or makes sure that they are in the library. The teacher sets the purposes of the unit (although the teacher may have the pupils set the purposes). The pupils go through projects, readings and writings, and they learn some preordained facts. A work unit may be reasonably open, but it tends to be fairly rigid because the teacher knows in advance what the work unit is designed to teach.

The theme is different. The teacher knows the skills that the children must develop--reading, writing, spelling, computation, etc. The teacher knows what concepts the children must come to understand as they develop skills--the alphabetic principle of written language, the spelling patterns found in words, the laws and patterns of mathematics.

The materials that are used in doing this are of little consequence. It matters not, in learning to count, whether children count stones or leaves or horses or bones in the body. In beginning work with the theme, the teacher does not know what will be counted--but does know that the children must learn the skill of counting and the concept of number.

With a single theme, the teacher knows further what concepts beyond skill development are to be gained. The teacher may want to develop the concept that physical well-being is related to diet--the concept that basic needs of food, clothing, and shelter are pervasive of most cultures even though people eat different foods, wear different clothing, or live in different-looking houses.

With the theme, the teacher collects the materials necessary to motivate and *begin*. The teacher knows what skills must be taught, but not how the theme will end, or even in what direction that the theme will go.

For example, one of the common themes for primary grades is Myself. (*See pages 31-36.*) The teacher knows that children are interested in themselves and hopes that they can be motivated into weeks of investigation about themselves.

The teacher knows that language will grow informally as the children work together, but the teacher also will want to stimulate it somewhat formally during a part of each day.

The theme will allow for, and almost require, that all children do some work in reading, writing, math, art, and music. The teacher will begin by teaching the total group. For several weeks, part of each day may be devoted to total-group instruction, and many of the activities will require total-group participation. A major share of all work will be oral; as a general rule, oral readiness (discussion to motivate and to build concepts) precedes all activities.

For language, the children talk about themselves and their likes, as suggested in the previous chapter. They talk about these things at great length, with the teacher directing the discussion and channeling ideas, with the teacher reacting and changing the direction or the emphasis of the ideas or activities when something catches the imagination of the children. The children make drawings to represent their ideas, and they write about their ideas. They read each other's drawings and writings, and they respond to each other's ideas. They may also dramatize their feelings or their ideas.

The children discuss their own shapes and sizes. They may weigh themselves and measure themselves. They may count and make graphs showing how many children have blue eyes, green eyes, black eyes, etc.; how many boys there are and how many girls; how many have curly hair, how many have straight hair; how many have older brothers or older sisters; what size their shirts, shoes, etc., are. The equipment and materials for making measurements and for recording the results are in the math center, which is one of several subject centers in the classroom.

In working with the theme of **Myself**, the children may discuss the kinds of homes in which they live, the kinds of rules that govern their actions, the kinds of communities in which they live. (The social studies center may be filled with reference materials about other kinds of homes and other kinds of communities so that they may study these and make comparisons.) They may make maps of their communities or plans of their houses. (Here the social science activities overlap the math activities, while language runs throughout.

It is not possible to make rigid distinctions between the different interest centers.)

Educational openness means being ready to stimulate all of the preceding activities, but even more it is being sensitively observant of the responses of the children, recognizing their interests, and shifting the activities to follow their interests. For example, as the children begin to try to measure their bodies, they may become fascinated by the history of measurement, or the ways in which we can measure. They may learn ways of linear measurement, measurement of volume, measurement of weight, or even density. They may become interested in meters, use a meter stick, and discover the common aspect of a thermometer, pedometer, speedometer, odometer, barometer, hydrometer, etc. It is highly unlikely that any of these discoveries will occur without teacher impetus, response, and provision of materials and equipment.

In one first-grade class, the children researched the history of measurement, and several children made books to record their findings. One child produced the following. It is typical of the work that several children did.

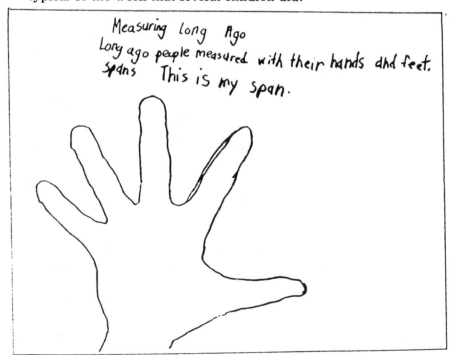

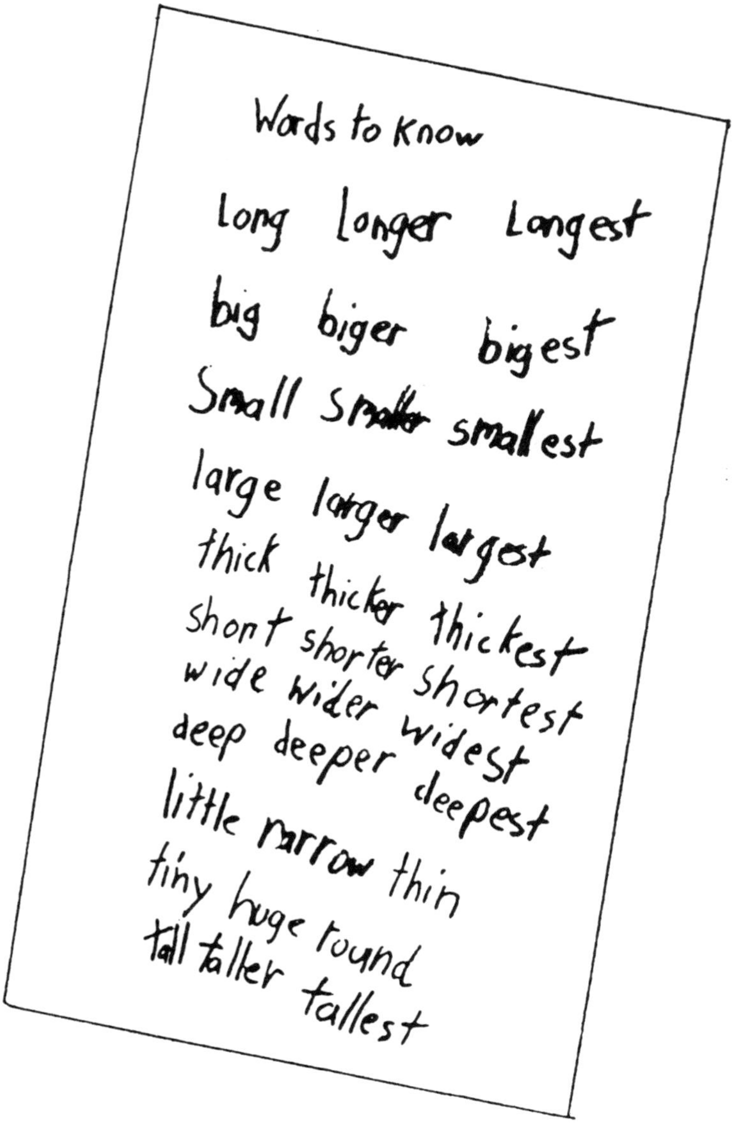

Words to know

long   longer   Longest

big   biger   bigest

Small   Smaller   smallest

large   larger   largest
thick   thicker   thickest
shont   shorter   shortest
wide   wider   widest
deep   deeper   deepest
little   narrow   thin
tiny   huge   round
tall   taller   tallest

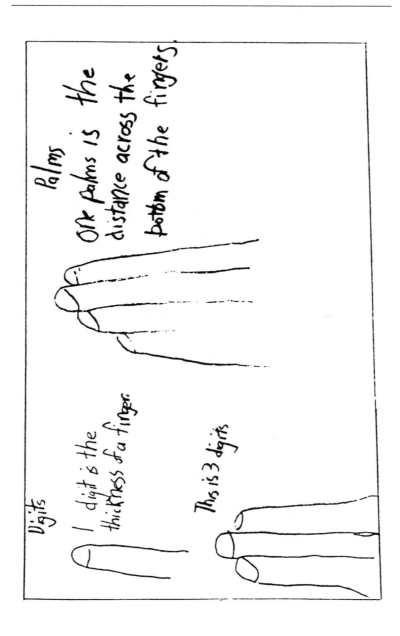

Palms

One palm is the distance across the bottom of the fingers.

Digits

1 digit is the thickness of a finger.

This is 3 digits

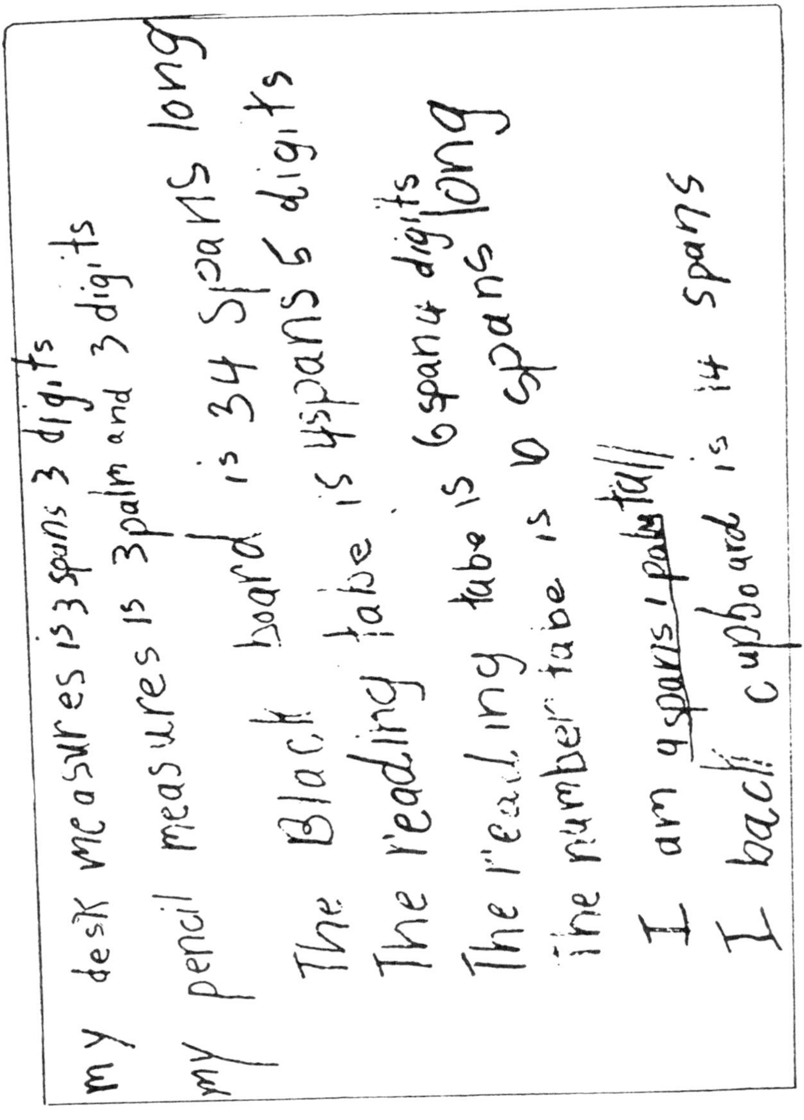

my desk measures is 3 spans 3 digits

my pencil measures is 3 palm and 3 digits

The Black board is 34 spans long

The reading tabe is 4 spans 6 digits

The reading tube is 6 span 4 digits

The reading tube is 0 spans long

the number tube is 0 spans long

I am 9 spans 1 palm tall

I back cupboard is 4 spans

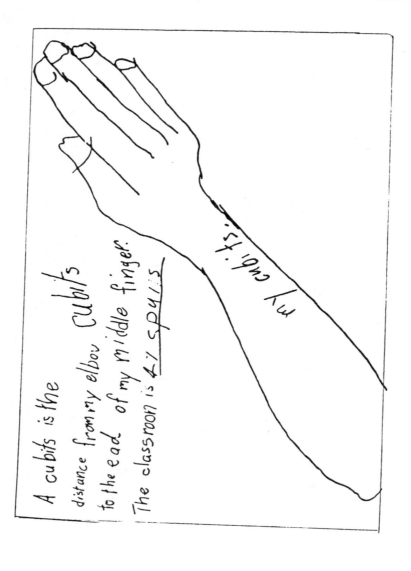

A cubits is the
distance from my elbow CUbits
to the ead of my middle finger.
The classroom is 47 cubits

my cubit.

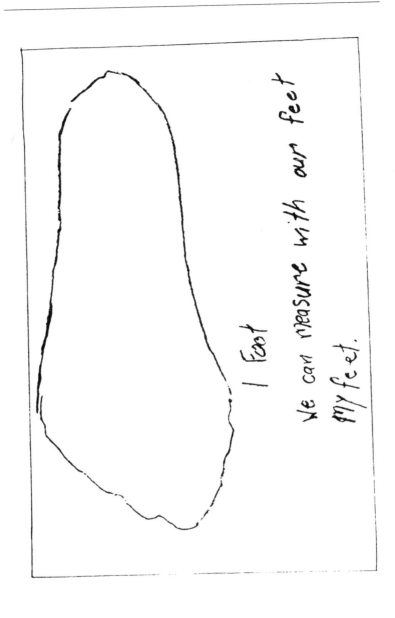

My head is 1 foot inches round.

My neck is 20 _____ inches round.

My chest is 37 _____ inches round.

My waist is 23 _____ inches round

My wrist is 6 _____ inches round

My hips are _____ inches round

My ankle is 27 _____ inches round

My ankle is 8 _____ inches round

The elephants tusks are 1 foot
Indian elephants grow ten feet
high.

The Wingspans of Birds

Snowy owl 5 feet = 5 rulers

Robin 9 inches

Blue Jay 15 inches = 1 foot 3 ins.

Herring Gull 51 inches = 1 foot 45 ins

Eagle 2 yards 1 foot = 7 feet

Albatross 3 yards 2 feet = 9 feet

3 | 3 | 4

Miles

Deas Tunnel ½ mile

Lulu Island about 12 miles long

Victoria 73 miles   San Francisco 993 miles

Nanaimo 41 Miles

Bellingham 57 miles San Francisco's Furthest from

Fort Langley 30 miles

Seattle 163 miles   Victoria is nearest to

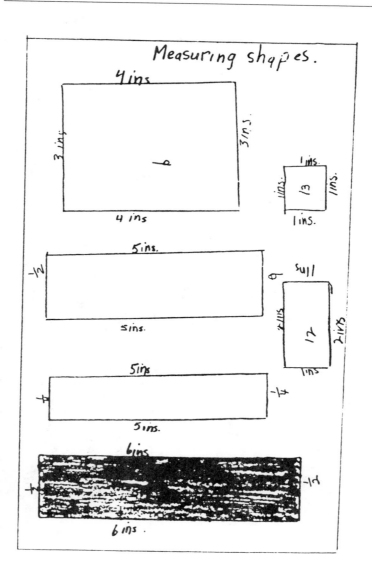

The children's study of their own voices may lead them to feeling their vocal chords, and thence to tuning forks or other vibrating instruments. They may move to a consideration of stringed instruments, string lengths, string thicknesses, and string tension and the effect of these upon sound. The children may observe the vibrations of a telephone receiver and a loudspeaker; they may study waves and wavelengths.

Books, of course, are needed throughout this study-- good, thick, authoritative reference books--books that are traditionally considered too difficult for children to read. The teacher guides the children as they use the books, skillfully providing the children with concrete experiences so that they can understand concepts as they discover answers.

These investigations might occur if the children were left alone with materials and time to investigate, but a teacher can guarantee that these kinds of investigations do occur if the teacher will teach, motivate, and openly respond to the children.

One kindergarten teacher exemplified this openness of teacher response when the teacher and the children produced the following poem. The teacher had not set out to produce a poem. (A work unit on poetry would have had this as a goal.) The theme was Fall, and the emphasis was on responding to the seasonal changes with all five of the common senses. The teacher wrote:

"We had been classifying leaves according to color, texture, number of points, etc. One of the girls crumpled her leaves and made a collage. The others joined in, making lovely pictures and beautiful abstracts. During this time, I asked them how the leaves affected their senses. We talk a lot about our senses--use them all the time! This is what came out of it."

We see leaves.
We see green, red, brown, yellow, pretty.

Leaves feel like fluffy cotton. . .
Crunchy like potato chips.
Some leaves feel stickery, like prickly cornflakes.
Some leaves sting like a bee.
Some feel ugly.

Cornflake leaves sound like crunchy, munchy candy.

Leaves have smells like rug and paste.
Some smell good.
Some smell bad.
Some smell red.
Some smell like outside.

Some leaves taste like meat, but not very often.
Leaves taste yucky.
They taste sour.
Some leaves taste almost sweet.

3. Attention span.

Teachers often complain about the short attention span of their pupils, and many studies have indicated that children have a very short attention span. Yet the authors' observations indicate that this is not necessarily so--that attention spans are much more related to *interest* than they are to age.

The authors have seen countless classes in September with pupils bouncing inattentively from one activity to another activity. Yet these same pupils four weeks later have maintained attention for fifty minutes in discussion and for another fifty minutes in independent writing or drawing.

Furthermore, millions of American children sit glued to the television screen at home, watching all the way through a long program that interests them. And certainly children can play in sand or water contentedly for hours at a time.

The fact seems to be that children (as well as adults) have a very long attention span when they are learning something that really interests them. The authors have observed some twenty kindergarten classes (classes labeled "disadvantaged," "nonlingual," or "hyperactive") listen to and dramatize *The Five Chinese Brothers*, as described on page 79. They attended to the project for sixty to ninety minutes consecutively. These were the children who at other times had been observed being hyperactive from boredom--nonlingual for lack of anything to say--disadvantaged from being required to try to do meaningless assignments.

The authors have also observed one class of dull, low-tracked, inattentive seventh-grade students discuss one page of *The Five Chinese Brothers* for a full fifty-minute period without losing enthusiasm, without behaving as if they were dull, low-tracked, or inattentive. The teacher's very sensitive response to one pupil's query about the word *extraordinary* triggered the discussion. To focus on this word had not been planned, nor had the teacher expected the book to last for all of the period.

One fourth-grade class of low-tracked Chicano pupils spent thirty minutes discussing what a cloud might look like from above. Not one of these children had ever been above a cloud. Perhaps this lack of experience was a blessing in that it stimulated the children's imagination. Furthermore, there was the advantage that there was no "right" answer.

Teachers who wish to maintain long attention spans in their classes must meet certain conditions. The material to be learned should not be too easy nor impossibly difficult; otherwise, boredom will take over. Children must be motivated to learn; what they are learning must appear to be relevant or stimulating to the imagination.

Perhaps most important of all, the teacher must be highly sensitive to spontaneous developments and flexible enough to "pick up the ball and run with it." If children are having a useful learning experience, the teacher must go along with them--even though the children are not learning what the teacher had planned for them. (There will always be another day for that.) Interest and attention are too valuable to sacrifice for the sake of a lesson plan.

4. The disadvantaged child.

The authors have an extreme dislike for the word *disadvantaged* because they feel strongly that labeling a child with this term creates tremendous obstacles to his learning. The authors are convinced that if we can forget that a disadvantaged child is disadvantaged and remember that he is a child, we usually can teach him.

There are, of course, children who might be labeled advantaged. Their spoken English is so close to standard English that they have a momentary linguistic advantage over children whose accents or dialects are pronounced. But the chief advantage with the advantaged child is that the teacher accepts him as a child who is readily teachable, and the teacher proceeds to teach him.

The child who speaks nonstandard English is accepted by the teacher as disadvantaged. The teacher assumes, often unconsciously, that the child can learn very little. And that is what happens--the child does learn very little. The teacher does, however, ordinarily show great compassion for such a child and tries hard to make the child feel happy, or at least comfortable.

Those who plead for child happiness as a prerequisite to learning have some justification for their view, but they forget that learning can beget happiness. And children are rarely happy for long in situations where the teacher is chiefly involved in amusing them.

Practically all children (except those who are severely mentally or emotionally handicapped) *want* to learn. And if the teacher really believes that a child can learn, this is what will usually happen.

Victor Beez's study of a mini-teaching program dramatically exposed unconscious attitudes of teachers and the effect of these attitudes upon children's achievement.[7] He worked with sixty Head-Start youngsters and sixty certified teachers. Each teacher was to teach one child twenty words. There was a single instructional period, and the experiment had excellent controls to rule out the effect of extraneous variables or causes of difference.

Beez randomly labeled each child as "bright" or "dull," with thirty as "bright" and thirty as "dull." He assigned pupils randomly to teachers and told the teachers how each child was labeled.

The results were as might be expected. The "bright" children learned more than the "dull" children. The "bright" children learned 30 percent of the twenty words, and the "dull" children learned 16 percent of the twenty words.

Fortunately, Beez had observed very carefully what happened during the teaching. There was one major difference. When a teacher had a "bright" pupil, the teacher spent the instructional period teaching. When a teacher had a "dull" pupil, the teacher taught little, and spent a large proportion of the period making the child feel happy or accepted.

The teachers' attitudes did not seem to affect learning, but they did affect *how much* the teacher taught. The teachers of the "dull" pupils actually did not even try to teach more than about half as many words as the teachers of the "bright" pupils tried to teach. The "bright" children learned 56 percent of what they were taught; the "dull" children learned 55 percent of what they were taught. (The "dull" children were, of course, just as "bright" as the "bright" children.)

It appears that being labeled as disadvantaged almost assures that a child will not learn because teachers unconsciously abdicate their role as teacher and assume the role of mother, friend, psychologist, etc. Ray Rist's longitudinal study of Harlem children with black teachers affirms this conclusion and seems to eliminate racial prejudice as the cause.[8] Prejudice is a cause, but it is not racial prejudice. It is prejudice connoted by the word *disadvantaged*, and it permeates the attitudes and actions of teachers.

Some teachers are well aware of the "self-fulfilling prophecy," and they try to avoid it. They avoid looking at pupil records (cumulative files) until they have worked with the class for at least a month. This can usually be achieved by explaining the reason to the principal of the school.

* * *

Reading is one part of communication--a skill that is based upon thinking. It should be obvious that thinking does not require a white skin, family affluence, nor standard English expression. The authors have taught successfully Japanese-Americans, Black Americans, Chicanos, Filipino-Americans, Tar-Heel Americans, French-Canadian Americans, and Native-Americans with the RIOTT approach. The differences in these children are minimal; the likenesses are great. For the most part, only common sense is needed to make the necessary teaching adaptations.

For example, French-Canadian American first-grade children may say *dese, dem,* and *dose* for *these, them,* and *those.* They may say *mudder* for *mother,* i.e., corresponding to the three American-English phonemes /t/, /d/, and /ð/, these children have only two, /t/ and /d/; since /ð/ is voiced and similar to /d/, they tend to use /d/ wherever /ð/ is required. The teaching of encoding requires these children to learn that their /d/ sound is encoded in two ways: *d* as in *dog, date,* and *mud*; *th* /ð/ as in *these* and *mother.* We may want to correct the *dese* to *these,* but if we try to do it before communicating , we will prevent their talking and stifle their learning.

Sometimes teachers are confused about what standard English really is, and the fault is not theirs. Most basal reading manuals say that the sound at the end of *candy, happy,* and *usually* is a "short" /i/. It is a short /i/ sound for a small segment of the American Midwest. It is shown as a long /e/ in some dictionaries, and most Americans tend toward the long /e/ sound.

The obvious answer to this dilemma is to teach ending *y* according to local speech patterns. Teachers who do this have no particular difficulty, except for changing the answer key for their workbooks.

This is but a minor example of the kind of flexibility that teachers exercise in fitting the education to the child.

5.   Teaching spelling, punctuation, and written grammar.

Children must learn spelling, punctuation, and written grammar, and all three must be taught if they are to be learned. The timing of the teaching and of the demand for mastery are, however, matters of priority and developmental expectation.

We don't expect children to speak in sentences with perfect articulation the first time they speak--nor the second, third, fiftieth, or thousandth time. We do expect children to learn to speak over a period of years, and they *do* master their spoken language as well as it is spoken around them.

The same expectations hold for mastery of written language. As stated in previous chapters, emphasis in the RIOTT program is upon conveying meaning and responding to messages conveyed. Very simple messages can be conveyed in writing with grossly inaccurate spelling, punctuation, or grammar. But children should be encouraged to do their best to convey their messages clearly and precisely (in the finished draft of their work). This emphasis upon clarity and precision leads naturally to the learning of writing conventions that enable our messages to be understood.

Spelling, punctuation, and written grammar are all conventions. Their logic can be understood, and they can be learned reasonably well over a period of six to eight years. We teach the child to correct what is preventing him from communicating in writing, and we then require him to use properly what he has been taught.

Teachers should reteach and correct until the child has mastery of a specific convention. Some of this is guess-and-try; the teacher guesses from the children's responses that they are ready for a certain learning and then teaches it. If the learning takes more than two reteachings, it would seem best to postpone the learning of that convention until a later date.

For example, children want to use the word *because* very early in their writing. It can be misspelled (phonetically and readably) *bekuz, becuz,* or *becos.* This word causes special problems because many children hear it as two words, *be* and *cause.* Since children generally pronounce *cause* as *cuz,* they find the word *because* very difficult to spell. The teacher, noting the need for the word, can teach it as a sight-spelling word, teaching that *because* is one word, and observing the phonetic regularity of *be* and the /k/ sound if "hard" *c* has been taught. Thereafter, *because* may be listed on a Useful Writing Words Chart, posted where it is always ready for easy reference. From then on, the correct spelling of *because* is demanded.

Similarly, when children are hearing vowel sounds well, they can be asked to think of all the words they can in which they hear the sound of long /a/. These words are written correctly as the children dictate. Each word should be written on a separate 3" x 5" or 3" x 8" card and given to the child who thought of it.

The words may be sorted by the group, and in doing this the children can discover spelling patterns that they can begin to use as they write. The children should discover that the long *a* and other "long" vowels have spelling patterns, for example:

1. *a*-consonant-*e*, as in *ate*
2. *ay* at the end of words, as in *may*
3. *ai*, as in *pail*
4. *ei*, as in *weigh*.

The children probably will discover these four patterns, as well as several others that are used less frequently. The children will also probably discover that they must learn the word *they* as an irregular word since the *ey* it uses to represent the long /a/ sound is not found in many words that first-grade children think of.

This soliciting of words and developing an understanding of their spelling patterns may take two weeks, with fifty minutes a day spent on thinking, discussing, and classifying. (This time factor is mentioned because some teachers who have read this suggested approach have tried to complete the activity in one hour. When this is done, the activity fails because the children do not have enough time to think, to assimilate, to produce enough words, nor to discover the patterns. This activity may also fail if the teacher does too much telling, rather than eliciting in securing completion of the investigation.)

It may be that a study of homophones will develop from *made* and *maid*, *eight* and *ate*, etc. Once children realize that the long /a/ is almost always signaled by some additional letter or letters, the teacher no longer accepts *ma* for *may*, nor *cak* or *kak* for *cake*. The teacher might accept *mai* or *meigh* for *may*. The teacher might accept *caik* or *cayk* for *cake*. (Admittedly, these examples of misspelling are the authors' and are unlikely to be spellings chosen by the children.)

Somewhat surprisingly--although teachers should have enough faith in children not to be surprised--when children spell phonetically they tend to spell correctly without knowing that they are correct and without knowing why. For example, *wait* is spelled *wait*, not *wate*. *Potato* is spelled *potato*, *putato*, or occasionally *putatoe*, but very rarely *potayto* or *potaito*.

This may reflect an unconscious response to words that the children have seen in print, but it seems to occur naturally before children are looking much at words in programs that emphasize spelling and writing without SSR or some similar training. Paradoxically, when teachers stress digraphs in order to get correct spelling, children begin to follow rules rather than instinct. They then may produce *poataytoe* or *poetaiteoe*, *goe* or *goa* for *go*, and even *mee* and *wee* for *me* and *we*.

Some children will want to look up words in dictionaries if they are worried about the correctness of their spellings (which some children are). But a demand that children look up words for spelling creates a disinterest in writing for many children. An early emphasis upon dictionaries, particularly picture dictionaries in the first and second grades, seems to retard spelling skill. Children begin to depend consciously upon their eyes, rather than their ears. At this stage in a child's education, spelling is usually primarily a listening skill.

Many children will learn the basic elements of punctuation almost unconsciously. They will notice that capital letters are used in books to begin sentences and that most sentences end with a period. When these conventions are understood, they are usually used in writing. Correct punctuation should then develop gradually, with only an occasional review or correction needed. When children are concerned with communication, they want to learn writing conventions that enable them to communicate clearly. Conventions are learned and used without being stressed by the teacher. When conventions are emphasized to the diminution of ideas and communication, they seem never to be learned or used automatically.

Throughout school, children are exposed to standard written conventions of spelling, punctuation, and grammar through books. As children develop auditory sensitivity to language, they become increasingly aware of how oral language is encoded.

All this learning takes time, years of time, and it is hard work. But if a teacher can maintain emphasis upon communication while remaining sensitive to each child's level of development--demanding of each child as much as he has learned, as much as he can be taught--this kind of learning will usually take place.

There are, of course, no magic formulas for producing correct spelling, punctuation, and written grammar, but one very important principle is involved. *Communication* is always more important than *convention*, except in tests on convention.

6. Beginning the program.

In theory any program should work best if children begin the program when they start school and proceed with it year after year. But the RIOTT program does not have to begin in any particular grade because most of it is readily usable in any grade--without prerequisites.

The teacher begins with the pupils' experiences, develops their thoughts about themes based upon their experiences, and gets children responding orally and in writing so that the levels of skill development can be observed.

Each child's skill development begins or continues from *where he is*, not from *where he is supposed to be*. Children read books in SSR, and discussion grows naturally.

The RIOTT program begins whenever a teacher chooses to begin, and it ends if that teacher or next year's teacher uses a different program. In contrast, a tightly structured program requires tightly controlled sequential exercises. Switching children in or out of tightly structured programs is often very difficult. The RIOTT program does not create this difficulty.

The RIOTT program does not need to be imposed in total upon a class. Small parts of it can be added to complement most programs. For example, the writing of journals or SSR are natural complements to practically any language program. As complements, they do take time, and time in the school day is at a premium. But the practicing of skills, the development of thinking, the enjoyment of language, and the use of books can hardly be considered antithetical to either traditional or newer language programs.

Perhaps the large amount of independent work generated in the RIOTT program that goes unmarked, uncorrected, or unrewarded by a grade or a gold star may be viewed as antithetical to some structured programs based upon interpretations of Skinnerian principles of behavior modification. The authors feel, however, that extrinsic rewards are frequently not the real reinforcement.

The real reinforcement is the inner satisfaction that is apparent as children write independently, as well as the children's understanding that they are communicating with an author when they read silently. This is reinforcing in the sense that B.F. Skinner meant that it should be. The reinforcement is contiguous with the child's response. It is intrinsic and therefore self-perpetuating.

The RIOTT program can develop in many different ways. The authors have used the theme Myself in kindergarten through the eighth grade, and they have seen and read of successful versions of this theme in high schools and colleges. The forms of expression vary, and the activities vary. They vary primarily in the level of sophistication and in the amount of time given to a single theme. The theme Myself has evolved into the writing of autobiographies and biographies. The authors have even seen Myself evolve into a complex course in physiology and biology.

The method of using frames has proved successful at all levels, kindergarten through the eighth grade (*I like* _____ or *I want to be* _____). The authors have used George Mendoza's marvelous poem *And I Must Hurry for the Sea Is Coming In*[9] from the second grade through graduate school. From it the frame, *When I am a man I shall be* _____, was used to develop poems similar to Mendoza's prologue.

The authors have seen themes and responses develop for an hour, a day, a week, or a month. For those teachers who want to sample the RIOTT program, time and effort are the only demand. A small sampling of the program does not require teachers to abandon their current programs--programs that are functioning well and in which they feel secure. The authors have found that most teachers are very successful when they sample judiciously. Often the demand from the pupils to continue brings about further sampling and eventually full implementation.

Also the authors have found that sometimes teachers become enthusiastic too fast and plunge so deeply that they must backtrack. This backtracking is most common with those teachers who want environmental or behavioral openness to manifest too quickly. The greatest success occurs with those teachers who open their classes educationally and who allow the behavioral and environmental openness to evolve slowly--and only to the degree acceptable to the community and school administration.

Overall, there is a high rate of acceptance of the RIOTT program when teachers focus on educational openness. Most principals are supportive of children's reading silently in an SSR activity, and most parents accept SSR. It is necessary to explain that SSR is the *drill* of silent reading, not the teaching of reading, since occasionally a parent who misses the explanation complains about children's "wasting time" in school reading silently when they should be being "taught." In one community, a fifth-grade teacher called the program SRD, "silent reading drill." Diplomatic introduction obviously eases the establishing of an innovative program.

The authors have found that principals and parents are supportive of journals and writing. There are some problems about the teachers' not correcting spelling and grammar, but most of this can be explained amicably, and is probably best done when the program begins. The following journal is a good example of student writing; it is detailed and creative. Parents who can see their children's work in an attractive format recognize the competence of the teacher.

That I was gone so
I trnd around with the
Balloons and I saw my
Mom looking for me
My hands were cold
So I put my hand in
The poket I felt

Something in my Poket
it pokte me and I
took it out it was a
Neadl I was almost to
the grownd so I popt
One of the balloons
Then I was down on the
grownd the end

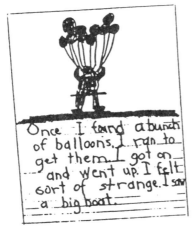

Once I fornd a bunch
of balloons. I ran to
get them I got on
and went up. I felt
sort of strange. I saw
a big boat.

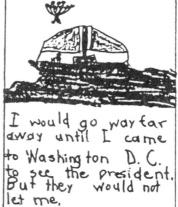

I would go way far
away until I came
to Washington D. C.
to see the president.
But they would not
let me.

Then I got tired
and tried to go home
and caught a plane
and went home.

The End
by Geoffrey Atwill

In the first grade, the spelling problem is not a problem at all, since most children begin writing almost immediately and most parents are pleased that their children can write at all. One teacher assuaged an angry mother by the simple, honest statement that her child's spelling was phonetic and that the child's writing (with nonstandard, uncorrected spelling) was part of a phonics program. It is difficult to imagine a more diplomatic stroke in teacher-parent relations.

Teachers using the RIOTT program will understand why they teach as they do, and therefore they can usually explain it successfully to parents. When parents discover professional competence in a teacher, they are ordinarily supportive rather than negatively critical. (There will always be a few parents who will want their children to be taught the way they themselves were taught, but sometimes these parents are won over by their children's enthusiasm about what is happening at school--enthusiasm based upon the true joy of learning.)

It is to be expected that some teachers will create their own adaptations of the program. One teacher who did this in September wrote to the authors in November as follows: "Thought you might be interested in what my group of eighth-graders think of 'S.S.R.' and 'Journals.' I have them for two periods--listed as English and U.S. History. I feel this approach is fantastically successful."

I think journels are a real good thing. It let's you express your thoughts. I think 2 pages is enough to wright. S.S.R. makes you so you can read more and alot better. I think I read alot more than I once did. It is kind of different from anything else that you do in school. I hope we will continue to do this all year. This is much better than doing English like verbs, adverbs, nouns, pronouns, I had enough of that last year. I seem to want to wright more than I once did. Every week I wright almost everything I know. I really do enjoy it!

* * *

I think it is a lot of fun Writing in my journal cause I have never had to write a journal before. I also like the S.S.R. time too.

* * *

I like S.S.R. and Writing in jernels too. and I like learning to read to too.

* * *

S.S.R.
I think that the Reading helps people read more books but sometimes they get tired of reading and they want to do something else
Journal
I think the journal helps improve writing it also sometimes brings up there imagination and there thoughts of what they want to explore and investigate in the world

* * *

I like the reading both what we read ourselves and what you read. I don't like writing in a journal because sometimes I can't think of what to write.

* * *

S.S.R.

I think it is a very good idea. I read a lot more than I used to. I used to just hate reading but now I sort of look forward to the next reading time.

Journals

I can write a lot better than I used to.

*   *   *

Reading

I think that it is kind of nice but some days I don't feel like reading a book, so I think you should be able to read mag. too.

S.S.R.

I like it and feel that it has helped to answer questions better in other classes.

*   *   *

Journels

Will I suppose it's good at least to me it is. It unloads your mind. If you have a problem just write it down + it sort of clears up your mind it also relaxes you.

S.S.R.

I like it because you learn to enjoy reading much more you are able to read better and to comprehend better in silence.

*   *   *

My Opinion

I like S.S.R. because I like reading because it helped me reed faster.

writting in my Jernal helps me understand words better. and it helps my writting a lot better. So I think that we should keep on reeding in the class room and keeping on writting.

*   *   *

In silent reading its OK I've learned by this method to read faster and better than what I ever had in writting I really can't say much because I really don't know if I've improved or not because I really hate writting. I do it though because it's an assignment and I have to turn it in to the teacher to get a grade out of her.

* * *

I like when we read. I used to hate to read because there weren't many chances I got to read. But now it's all so different. I've read 4 or 5 books and I'm reading one now. Last year at this time I had only read 1 or 2.

I like writing too, but there are some days when I can't write very much. Sometimes I have alot to write and then its time to write I forget all that I wanted to write. That get's some people mad when they do that. When I do that I think of something else. (Anyway I try.)

I also like when you read to us. Because the stories are interesting.

* * *

I never used to read like I do now. I have read 2 1/2 books so far and hope to read more. I like the S.S.R.

I am now getting used to writeing alot more then what I used to do.

When Mrs Larson reads to us we listeing to her and we learn about some histery to.

* * *

I like journals but I don't like reading, because I get tired. I read the news paper more than I did, but I don't like to read books. I think its all right that you read in front of class. But I like you to read some mysterys. I like lots of shocking ecitement. Like frankenstein and stuff like that.

* * *

S.S.R.
I don't like it to much but I do read more books last year I only read a few books a used them for book reports.

Writing in Journals
I guess it's all right one good thing about it is that I have to remember what happened in so I can write in the journal.

Your Reading Out loud
I don't like it very much but it takes up time that we could be doing other work and thats good.

* * *

S.S.R.
first I'm going to say what I think about uninteruped sustaned silent reading.

I think It has helped me alot, I have read alot more books than I use to and It has helped me to have a better understanding of things It gives us kids alot more freedom and at the same time we are injoying it as we learn.
second I will tell what I think if wrighting in jornals. At first I didn't think It was any good but once you got use to it, it is very fun and you get a chance to wright what you feal.

* * *

Mrs. Larson now that I am in here I can I think read better and faster than what I could befor because you know I was in Mrs. ------- class Last year for reading and she helped alot. Well now for the journal I like writing in them very much and I feel as if I am taliking to my mom and I have talked to alot of people and told them my feelings twords you and they say a Teacher and laugh at me

* * *

I like the S.S.R. I seme to be reading more at home. I uslay don't read unless i have to. I like the deal about the gernel it not that hard and you can say whats on your mind and what you fell like a hippy frend of mine every one shed let it all come out at one time or anouther. and about the reading in class i think its pertty cool cuse you can just sit back and lisen and lern somethink at the same time.

*　　*　　*

S.S.R.
I think that its a *good* idea. I've read more books this year than I have read all my life. Only I wish we had *just* a little more time to read our books. I get to an interesting part + then we have to quit. Oh well!

*　　*　　*

Righting in the jernals helped me to right better and when we do english assignements out of a book isn't very fun to do. The reading seemed to make me read more books that I wouldn't have the time fore. When we read out of a book it help us to learn more things. I like it when you read to us because nobody else dose it.

*　　*　　*

I Journal
I think its pretty cool. I've gotten a little better in my writing. Im still kinda sloppy, but its coming along I think its a real good thing to have houranls. We should have them all year. But next year we might get a little behind in English cause we haven't had too very much of it. Thats why I need it so badly.
II Reading to Us
It's O.K.
Thats All.

*　　*　　*

I read more and a understand it more and enjoy it
I write better and don't mind writing
S.S.R. is fun because now I don't try reading my book when I should be doing other school work, but, I'm not reading as many books or as much as I used to for some reason.

Writing in the journel is fun to but sometimes I can't think of anything to write!

Being read to is kind of boring especialy since what you read to us is always history. Johnny Tremain was interesting but you should read different kinds of books for variety.

*   *   *

S.S.R.

I like to read and normally, at school, I don't get much time to read. This time I read at school helps me to read better and faster. I get to read more books too.
Joural
I thought it was a waste of time at first, now I don't think that. That is because I find it easier to write things.

*   *   *

Well I think that I kinda like write this journal but I don't like your reading its boring you should read some exciting books instead of old history we get enough of that out of our history books I think we do. (more than enough)

I like spelling the way you do that and I think we should have some good old fashion spell downs those are fun well thats all Ive got to say.

*   *   *

I haven't been here very long but I think the Reading and the Journal are both a good Idea.

*   *   *

I like it and i thing I rede a lote mor now.
the jeebo is a lot of fun to but I Wish you wood gif a litte mor tine becos all of us ar not good rioters an thes all i got to sae.

*   *   *

S.S.R.

I guess it's OK exspessily when you got a book that you like and you want to read it but when I'm reading a book that I dont like it drags on and on. I don't really read any more or less cause I've always liked to read and I read a lot.

I guess writing in a jornel is OK not that I like it all the time.

*   *   *

I relly like S.S.R. becaus now I read. Befor S.S.R. I never even read hardly so it is helping me withe my reading. And you also get to pick the book you read you don't have to read out of the same Reading book day after day

I also like writing in jurnuls. Becaus I get a chanch to write what I want to write. And we don't have to use good punctuation or spelling. And It is funner then regular English

*   *   *

7. Lesson planning.

It is undoubtedly comforting to write in a lesson plan for Monday: "Reading, pages 128-136." In traditional teaching, this makes good sense. Page 127 was finished on Friday, so page 128 is the logical place to begin on Monday.

But what is the teacher who is following the RIOTT program going to write in the lesson plan book? Again, the answer depends to a great extent on what happened on Friday. Where were the children in their development of a theme? If they had not finished their work with the theme, there should be some recapitulation of what has happened so far in the development of the theme before picking up where they left off on Friday.

Perhaps new phonemes are to be presented. Perhaps the children are to continue their experiences in individual authorship. Whatever part of the program the children are working on, the learning process is continuous.

There are, of course, some things that happen every day. The children are expected to read silently in SSR every day. They are expected to write in their journals every day once they have begun writing journals. And, of course, the teacher will read orally every day. Still there are times when the teacher may be searching for new ideas--new things to do.

There are four prime sources of ideas:

1. other teachers working in the same program
2. the children in each class who by their reactions indirectly, sometimes directly, suggest additional units of thought or themes
3. professional books and periodicals
4. the teacher's own reading of children's books and asking, "What activity will this story generate?" "What theme will this story inspire?"

Invariably, concern about what to do next is resolved, but it tends to recur. Even the most creative teachers sometimes manifest this concern, perhaps because they are demanding of themselves or responding to the demands of the program, rather than copying someone else's ideas.

With the RIOTT program, large blocks of time and flexibility are required. This program is a total class program. Many parts of the program demand total class participation under the leadership of the teacher.

When the children become deeply interested, as they regularly do, then even having morning recess at a fixed time can create an undesired interruption. The authors regularly observe first-grade children working without an artificial break (for recess, for milk, or for music) for two to three hours. During this time children do change activities, from reading to writing to talking to drawing, as they pursue a theme. They may sing or dance as an outgrowth of the theme. Their activities have naturalness and spontaneity.

A teacher who must use the gymnasium from 10:15 to 10:40 has an impediment to the RIOTT program. A teacher who must send ten of the children to speech therapy at a fixed time has an impediment to the program. A teacher who cannot begin working before 9:15 without running the risk of being interrupted by routine announcements on the loudspeaker system has an impediment to the program.

A teacher who is scheduled to watch science on television three days a week at 11:00 has an impediment to the program. A teacher who must identify six children as remedial readers and send them out of the room for remedial reading has an impediment to the program. A teacher who must use an aide or student teachers in a prescribed way has an impediment to the program.

These are just some of the usual educational disruptions that plague every teacher--disruptions so common that the word *disruption* may seem inappropriate or offensive. But the authors do feel strongly that a teacher should be able to establish the time schedule for the class, with flexibility for changes as the children's activity indicates.

A remedial reading teacher may at first feel uncomfortable working in a RIOTT classroom, listening and participating rather than teaching--and then teaching those who need help rather than those who have been labeled as needing help. A music teacher may feel uncomfortable listening to a class, learning about its current theme, and working to provide musical experiences relevant to the theme rather than teaching at a specific time each day.

But specialists can work productively within the RIOTT program. They may spend less time in formal teaching and more time in providing materials, but the results are more gratifying.

A child may seem to get a better physical education by going to a gymnasium regularly, but a school with enough open space outside where the classes can go when they wish, or a school that permits "gym" within the classroom can be just as satisfactory. An in-classroom gym program has the advantage of eliminating the time impediment to the program.

The RIOTT program is viewed as a one-teacher-per-class

program. Even though it ir *.*vidualizes output, it does not accept the concept that one-to-one teaching is the epitome of education. There is a need for the one-to-one feeling, but the feeling of belonging individually and being appreciated individually does not necessarily come from one-to-one teaching.

While the authors can see some advantages in one-to-one teaching, there are obviously disadvantages. For one thing, the teacher in a one-to-one situation may do much of the work that should be done by the children. Children quickly learn to be dependent if there is someone readily available to ask, particularly if the someone is an adult who wants to teach. The authors have noted that in classes where the teacher-pupil ratio has been one-to-ten or less (achieved by having aides or student teachers in the room), the children quickly become dependent upon the adults to tell them how to spell, how to solve a problem, how to get the right answers, etc.

Another disadvantage of one-to-one teaching is that it stops or greatly diminishes the learning that flows spontaneously as children communicate with each other. Furthermore, a one-to-one teaching or one-to-ten teaching is much more expensive than a one-to-thirty or one-to-forty ratio.

The amount of space affects very definitely how many children a teacher can teach. Given even minimally adequate space, one teacher can handle thirty to forty pupils. In fact, when the number is large, the teacher must place more faith in the pupils' ability to learn alone and from each other. This faith is rewarded.

The most obvious disadvantage of large classes from the teacher's point of view is the inordinate amount of clerical work involved. Some of this clerical burden robs the teacher of time and energy that could be spent much more productively. Worse still, some of the clerical duties imposed upon teachers rob the children of learning time. This is something that our educational system can ill afford.

8.   Achievement.

Every educational program has some problems, and new programs may have more problems than established ones have. With the RIOTT program, one of the biggest problems is that many teachers worry about achievement. Will their pupils achieve? Will they do well on standardized tests?

Anybody who analytically observes a class in the RIOTT program can see that the children are achieving. It is clear that the children are thinking, writing, and reading. The children are enjoying language. Yet there is that niggling doubt about how well these children will do on standardized tests.

Although it may seem paradoxical, a standardized test is valid only to the degree that it does not reflect the specific teaching of a single word list, a single approach, or a single teacher. Most standardized tests are well constructed, and they are not susceptible to responding based upon a single type of teaching.

Standard reading tests are built upon certain assumptions. When these assumptions are rendered invalid, the results of the tests are invalid. But most of the assumptions are reasonable, and these assumptions can be met without restricting a teacher's teaching:

1. From a small sample of performance, we can infer achievement.
2. What we measure is a symptom of achievement, not the achievement. We infer achievement from the symptoms.
3. A child who can read books can recognize words in isolation or in short phrases and can understand words in isolation or short phrases.
4. A child who can read and discuss books can read short paragraphs with understanding.
5. A child who can read books and interpret their messages individually can read short passages, read questions based upon the passages, and select best answers among four or five answers, even though the child's individual answer is not one of the four or five available answers.

The makers of tests state clearly that there may be error in any test score, and they state that the amount of error likely will be greater in an individual child's score than in the class mean (average). Further, the norming of a standardized test is based upon normal statistics so that the average is a true midpoint, with half of the pupils scoring above the average and half below. We are saying that when we use ten thousand or more students as the sample, the median and the mean are essentially the same in the making of norms.

We cannot expect that all children taught under any program will be above average, nor should we judge a program's worth by expecting all class means to be above some norm group's average. If every class in a large school system scores above average on a single test, it probably means that the norms are invalid, although it could mean that the norming group achieved very poorly at the time the norms were developed.

A standardized test, or a series of standardized tests administered periodically, once or twice a year, will reflect the growth of a class. And it is the *amount of growth* that should be our concern--not the score at one point in time compared with some normative average.

Perhaps an analogy will help to clarify this. Bill was the smallest child in the class when he was weighed and measured in the first grade. He finished the twelfth grade weighing one hundred and twenty pounds and measuring sixty-four inches in height. He was healthy and had never missed a day of school because of illness. He was still the smallest boy in the graduating senior class. He was always below average and probably always will be below average in weight and height. But the concept of "below average" physique is essentially meaningless.

The concept of "below average" is just as meaningless in reading. See Figure 3. Note the standardized tests' normative average. Note Bill's regular progression. It is meaningless to worry about Bill's below-average achievement year after year so long as he is growing, and so long as we observe him reading, writing, and thinking. The difference between a reading achievement score of 12.0 and 11.0 is real but unnoticeable in a practical sense. The difference in Bill's height of sixty-four inches and the national norm is real but unnoticeable in the practical sense of living as an adult.

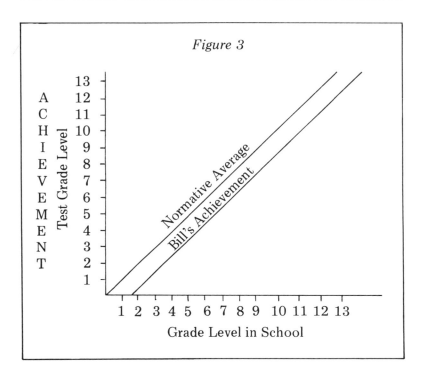

Figure 3

If we demanded that Bill play basketball, we could develop some real problems for him. No remedial program will make Bill seventy-two or seventy-six inches tall. If we demand that Bill or pupils like him must be above average in reading achievement at all times, or at any particular time, we will develop problems for him. Worse still, we may retard his normal, satisfactory development.

Children who are taught under any program in which they read books, write regularly, learn to work independently, and are encouraged to think will perform and score satisfactorily on standardized tests. There is no need to study specific word lists nor to practice on thousands of testlike work sheets labeled by comprehension skill areas in order to be able to do the test. Children trained under such drill programs may, and probably will score satisfactorily on standardized tests. There is little reason, however, to suppose that children who are trained in this way will also be able to think, read books, or write creatively to the extent that pupils trained with the RIOTT program can.

A simple example of nonreversible inference may help to explain this. Edward Dolch developed a word list during the 1930s based upon three word-count studies of frequency of word usage. He published the Dolch Basic Word List of 220 words in 1941. He and many others inferred that a child in learning to read would learn to read these 220 words.

This inference was and still is sensible. The authors consider this inference to be nonreversible, although it can be reversed. When reversed, it says that children should learn the 220 Dolch words in order to learn to read.

But it is impossible to teach a child to read and write without using the 220 Dolch words. If these words are used naturally, in meaningful contexts, the 220 words are learned, and the recognition of these 220 Dolch words is *then* a valid symptom from which we can infer that a child can read. If these 220 words are first taught in artificial contexts, or in isolation through drills and games, the recognition of the 220 Dolch words is no longer a valid symptom from which we can infer that a child can read.

Children who are taught to read with the RIOTT program will learn the 220 Dolch words. They will know the basic words on any test because basic words are basic to all communication. Besides, the children will learn hundreds or thousands of nonbasic words.

In considering achievement, it is important to keep in mind that an individual child's growth is sporadic in most developmental areas. A child may spurt in height or weight at particular times, but there are plateaus when a child does not seem to grow much at all. This same kind of sporadic growth occurs in reading, writing, and thinking.

The sporadic nature of growth may be more noticeable (and worrisome) under the RIOTT program than under other programs. A program with tight structure and weekly, monthly, or work-unit tests will give scores that imply regular growth and which give the teacher a feeling that rather regular increments of learning are being achieved.

Programs that teach ten words a week and test ten words a week give results from which we infer that learning is taking place. If the daily drills are intense and well structured, the results on Friday are good. The scores are high. But retention and meaningful application are another matter. The remedial classes that abound throughout the nation suggest that application and retention of tightly structured reading programs are not very high.

The authors' purpose here is not to condemn other programs, but to describe a phenomenon of achievement that they have observed frequently, particularly with children beginning to read or beginning the RIOTT program. Individual children and whole classes seem to perform on plateaus for several weeks, and children occasionally seem to perform at a plateau level for several months.

For example, in learning to discuss ideas, in generating thoughts in response to a question such as "What is red?" a class may seem bumbling and unresponsive for six, eight, or twenty lessons. On lesson twenty-one, however, the class comes to life; responses pour forth from all the children; and the teacher may even have to cut off the discussion at the end of an hour. Thereafter, hour-long discussions seem natural.

The authors have had several instances where children have discovered all of a sudden that they could read, write, or spell. James Herndon describes just such an occurrence in his Chapter "Harvey" in *The Way It Spozed to Be.*

> *Let me say clearly in advance that I don't know how Harvey learned to read. I don't know when he learned. I couldn't say this method worked or that one, whether phonics or word recognition, reading groups, flash cards, tape recorder, structural linguistics, or "Cowboy Small."*
>
> *On one of those last days, a commotion came from his reading group. I went over. Harvey stood up and announced to me, Mr. Hern-don, I can so read! Everyone jeered, with some justification. It wasn't as if Harvey had ever admitted he couldn't read.*
>
> *You go on and test me, Mr. Hern-don! cried Harvey. That was new, so I went over and got a copy of Red Feather. I turned to a page I was pretty sure he hadn't memorized and gave it to him. He held it standing up and, sure enough, began to read it. It was*

a section where Red Feather, the Indian boy, is learning to make arrows from the old arrow maker. I could remember reading it myself as a child. Harvey read about making the shaft straight by pulling it through a hole bored in a block of hardwood or a piece of sandstone, I can't remember which. He stumbled a little, stopped and puzzled, moving his lips, but he read it. Everyone knew he was reading, not just reciting something he knew by heart.

When he finished I said, We ought to give Harvey a hand. Everybody clapped and cheered; naturally there were a few calls of watermelon-head and chump mixed in. After the ovation Harvey couldn't shut up; he was in a daze. He kept talking like a reformed drunkard, telling about how bad things were when he couldn't read, how he knew all the letters, but put them together and they just didn't mean anything to him before, but now . . . and what he planned to read next . . .them comics . . . [10]

Delbert was another such first-grade pupil. Delbert had been in the RIOTT program in the first grade for three months. He had used very-own-words, drawn many pictures, participated in SSR using picture books, written several frame sentences, and had been responsive in discussion. He was considered by his teacher to be doing very well and would have ranked in the top five of his class of twenty-eight had such a ranking been made.

At ten o'clock one morning, Delbert came to his teacher individually and announced, "Mr. G., I can read."

"Yes, I know you can," said his teacher.

"No, Mr. G. I mean I can really read now. I couldn't when I came to school this morning, but I can now."

The teacher did not know what to say. He said nothing, so Delbert continued, "Look, I'll show you."

Delbert took the copy of *Charlotte's Web* from the teacher's desk, turned past Mr. G.'s marker, which noted the place where Mr. G. had stopped his oral reading. Delbert read a full page orally with only an occasional oral reading error.

"That's wonderful, Delbert," said Mr. G. "How did you learn?"

"I don't know for sure," said Delbert. "I have been thinking about reading, and this morning as I was thinking, I just knew I could read. It all makes sense, now."

Just as Herndon says, "Let me say clearly in advance that I don't know how Harvey learned to read," we don't know how Delbert learned to read, nor does Delbert. Delbert thinks that he knows when, but does he?

The authors have observed a sudden flowering of ability as late in the school year as June. William was a boy who had worked all year in the RIOTT program. He did all of his work with minimum success by normative standards and functioned well below all the other children in his class of thirty-eight. He was shy in talking, frequently couldn't think, and often could not give his very-own-word. He just looked at books during SSR, and he even had trouble getting his name printed correctly on his pictures--pictures that were immature.

One Tuesday in June, William wrote a full sentence to caption his drawing. The first letter was capitalized. The sentence ended with a period. On Wednesday William wrote a poem of four lines. He could write. He knew he could write. He was proud.

The authors have seen many children "learn" in this eureka fashion. The Delberts cause us no problem because they learn early. The Williams cause us great consternation because we fear they will never learn. We don't know when William learned. He may have learned in October or March. He did not manifest performing behavior until June.

Teachers must have faith in children and their ability to learn. Teachers must have faith that if they teach, and if the children participate regularly in reading, writing, and thinking activities, the behavioral manifestation will occur.

Many children, of course, progress without noticeable learning spurts or plateaus, but plateaus are common among the children. Plateaus are common among teachers too. They teach the RIOTT program for weeks, sometimes a year or more, and all of a sudden they know that they know what they are doing--and that they are doing it well.

If a district or school adopts a new program such as the RIOTT program by mutual agreement, teachers seem to be much less apprehensive about achievement. Having administrative support and colleagues with whom to share problems helps a lot.

Any program works best with active, interested supervisory support, and the RIOTT program is no exception. But basically it is the teacher, who lives and works with the pupils every day, who will make the program succeed. It is the teacher who must give the children the freedom to learn--and they *will* learn.

9.   Some Hard Data:

We have accumulated some test score data to indicate the success of children taught under RIOTT-like programs. The first is a ten year study of teachers and pupils in a federally funded program for minority-poverty children. All children were tested individually using the **Standard Reading Inventory** in April and May of grade two or three. Most of the pupils had been in the program for two or more years. They were a random sample of the total population drawn from twelve classrooms. See tables I and II for the results:

The data suggest several things. First, it takes three or four years before teachers develop enough facility with this sort of program to get maximum achievement. Second, minority members seem capable of normal, good achievement under a whole language program. The test scores at the beginning of the program were of the level "expected" of minority members. The scores at the end are unexpectedly high. This supports some of the notions described in the Beez, Rist, and Rosenhan studies. Thirdly, the data suggest that it is possible to teach with little or no failure. What the data do not show is that there were no non-readers during the last four years of the program. There were approximately 40% non-readers in the first two years of the program. We suggest that the merit of any program should not be how high the achievement average is, but the absence of failure.

We have the results of the Metropolitan Achievement Test for grade one in April of 1982 for a class funded federally as minority (Chicano and Appalachian). The data are reported for those pupils who entered grade one by November 1 of the 81-82 school year in Table III.

TABLE I

AVERAGE ACHIEVEMENT BY YEAR AND GRADE AS MEASURED BY THE STANDARD READING INVENTORY

GRADE 2

year	72	73	74	75	76	77	78	79	80	81
number	47	52	69	61	50	111	67	56	49	43
ave.	1.2	1.3	1.9	1.9	2.3	2.5	2.9	2.5	2.8	2.6

GRADE 3

number	—	38	44	52	36	114	61	46	40	36
ave.		1.7	2.8	3.0	3.1	3.2	3.6	3.9	3.3	3.9

TABLE II

PERCENTAGE OF PUPILS READING BELOW, ON, AND ABOVE GRADE PLACEMENT BY GRADE AND YEAR AS MEASURED BY THE STANDARD READING INVENTORY

GRADE TWO

year	72	73	74	75	76	77	78	79	80	81
below	77	69	54	48	44	27	21	23	12	19
on	11	17	15	20	16	17	24	18	18	14
above	13	13	32	33	40	49	55	59	70	67

GRADE THREE

below	—	68	42	52	36	37	21	13	25	8
on	—	32	48	25	36	29	44	37	45	32
above	—	0	11	27	28	34	34	50	30	60

TABLE III

PERCENTILE RANKINGS OF GRADE ONE PUPILS AS MEASURED BY THE METROPOLITAN ACHIEVEMENT TEST IN APRIL 1982

Percentile	Number of pupils	English as Second
90-99	4	0
80-89	12	5
70-79	0	0
60-69	1	0
50-59	1	1
40-49	3	1
30-39	1	0
1-29	0	0

We have mentioned that some pupils go through plateaus and make major leaps in achievement seemingly in one day when suddenly all the language learnings and practice reach fruition. We were able to test one group of children as they progressed through grades one and two measuring them individually with the **Standard Reading Inventory.** Sixteen children were available through the two year period. This was a small, rural school with a stable pupil population. Table IV gives the results.

TABLE IV

Whole Language Teaching Reading Achievement for 16
Pupils as Measured by the Standard Reading Inventory

level of reading (grade)	mid-grade one Jan 84	end grade one June 84	grade two April 85
failing to score	9	1	0
beginning	5	2	0
1	1	3	1
2	0	2	2
3	1	8	8
4	—	—	3
5	—	—	1
6	—	—	1
Average grade	0.61	2.74	3.93

There is evidence here, supported by informal testing and observation in other classes, that children in whole language programs go through a stage of muddling with language, making so many errors as they work that they fail to score on tests until they make a rather large leap, virtually vaulting from pre-primer muddling or failure to grade two or three achievement. This muddling period in grade one is a problem for some teachers and for many administrators who want to see measurable growth on tests at the end of every two or three months. The mastery tests of the basal reader programs are such tests since they provide tests at the end of the readiness materials, pre-primer, primer and first reader levels. We suggest that these tests measure skill format as practiced in the workbooks, not real reading skill. There are lots of observable evidences that the children reported above were learning, particularly their written journals and exercise books, and their ability to sustain themselves with books for long periods of silent reading.

We have reports of similar achievement from one California school required by state law to administer the California Achievement Test at the end of grade one. In a school with a 100% non-Anglo population the CAT scores average 3.7 to 3.9 at the end of grade one for a three year period. Prior to the use of a whole language program average scores were in the 1.5 range with rarely a single child score above 1.9. Under whole language a score below 2.0 is extremely rare. We take the achievement results to indicate that the standards on most standardized tests are much lower that we should anticipate if children received different instruction. The typical basal reader instruction confuses many children about print and reading and writing with the result that many children are turned into remedial reading candidates. In remedial reading they are likely to be taught more basal type material with extra skill emphasis and worksheets guaranteeing that they will remain crippled in language because they cannot understand and because they do not have the freedom to fail in order to learn.

1. Frank G. Jennings, *This is Reading* (New York: Bureau of Publications, Teachers' College, Columbia University, 1965), pp. 3-4.
2. Juniper Sage and Bill Ballantine, *The Man in the Manhole and The Fix-it Men* (New York: William R. Scott, 1952).
3. Claire Hutchet Bishop, illustrated by Kurt Wiese, *The Five Chinese Brothers* (New York: Coward McCann, 1938).
4. Florence Sawicki et al., "Key Words to Reading: The Language Experience Approach Begins," *Chandler Arizonian*, July 1969.
5. Charles Portis, *True Grit* (New York: Simon & Schuster, 1968).
6. Vernon Hale in *Teaching in the British Primary School*, ed. Vincent R. Rogers (New York: Macmillan, 1970), p. 131.
7. Victor Beez, "Influence of Biased Psychological Reports on Teacher Behavior and Pupil Performance," *Proceedings, 76th Annual Convention*, American Psychological Association, 1968, pp. 605-606.
8. Ray C. Rist, "Student Social Class and Teacher Expectations: The Self-Fulfilling Prophecy in Ghetto Education," *Harvard Educational Review* 40(3), August 1970, pp. 411-451.
9. George Mendoza, *And I Must Hurry For the Sea Is Coming In* (Englewood Cliffs, N. J.: Prentice-Hall, 1970).
10. James Herndon, *The Way It Spozed to Be* (New York: Simon & Schuster, 1968), pp. 177-178.

CHILDREN'S BOOKS MENTIONED IN THE TEXT

Aliki — *At Mary Bloom's*, New York: Greenwillow Books, 1976.

Bishop, Claire Hutchet. *The Five Chinese Brothers*. New York: Coward McCann, 1938.

Bright, Robert. *I Like Red*. Garden City, N. Y.: Doubleday & Co., 1955.

Carroll, Lewis. *Alice in Wonderland*.

Ginsburg, Mirra — *The Chick and the Duckling*, New York: MacMillan Publishers, 1972.

Green, Hannah. *I Never Promised You a Rose Garden*. New York: Holt, Rinehart & Winston, 1964.

Kipling, Rudyard. *Just-So Stories*.

Krauss, Ruth. *A Hole is to Dig*. New York: Harper & Row, 1952.

McCloskey, Robert. *Make Way for Ducklings*. New York: Viking Press, 1961.

————. *Time of Wonder*. New York: Viking Press, 1957.

McCracken, Marlene & Robert — *The Farmer and the Skunk, How do you say Hello to a Ghost*, — Tiger Cub Readers, Winnipeg: Peguis Publishers, 1986.

Mendoza, George. *And I Must Hurry For the Sea is Coming In*. Englewood Cliffs, N.J.: Prentice-Hall, 1970.

Moore, Clement. *'Twas the Night Before Christmas*.

North, Sterling. *Rascal*. New York: E. P. Dutton & Co., 1953.

O'Neil, Mary. *Hailstones and Halibut Bones*. Garden City, N. Y.: Doubleday & Co., 1961.

Piper, Watty. *The Little Engine That Could*. New York: Platt, 1930.

Portis, Charles. *True Grit*. New York: Simon & Schuster, 1968.

Potter, Beatrix. *Peter Rabbit*.

Sage, Juniper, and Ballantine, Bill. *The Man in the Manhole and The Fix-it Men*. New York: William R. Scott, 1952.

Sendak, Maurice. *Pierre*. Nutshell Library Series. New York: Harper & Row, 1962.

Shannon, George — *Lizard's Song*, New York: Greenwillow, 1981.
— *Dance Away*, New York: Greenwillow, 1982.

Twain, Mark. *Tom Sawyer*.

White, E. B. *Charlotte's Web*. New York: Harper & Row, 1952.

Anastasiow, Nicholas. *Oral Language: Expression of Thought.* Newark, Del.: International Reading Association, 1971.

Axline, Virginia. *Dibs: In Search of Self.* New York: Ballantine Books, 1967.

Beez, Victor. "Influence of Biased Psychological Reports on Teacher Behavior and Pupil Performance," *Proceedings, 76th Annual Convention,* American Psychological Association, 1968.

Blishen, Edward, ed. *The School That I'd Like.* Harmondsworth, Middlesex, England: Penguin Books, 1969.

Carlson, Ruth Kearney. *Sparkling Words.* Berkeley, Cal.: Wagner Printing Co., 1965.

Catterson, Jane H., ed. *Children and Literature.* Newark, Del.: International Reading Association, 1970.

Daniels, Steven. *How 2 Gerbils, 20 Goldfish, 200 Games, 2,000 Books and I Taught Them How to Read.* Philadelphia: The Westminster Press, 1971.

Fader, Daniel. *Hooked on Books.* New York: Berkley Publishing Corporation, 1968.

———. *The Naked Children.* New York: Macmillan, 1971.

Greer, Mary and Bonnie Rubenstein. *Will the Real Teacher Please Stand Up?* Pacific Palisades, Cal.: Goodyear Publishing Co., 1972.

Hall, Mary Anne. *Teaching Reading as a Language Experience.* Columbus, Ohio: Charles E. Merrill Co., 1970.

Henry, Mabel Wright. *Creative Experiences in Oral Language.* Champaign, Ill.: National Council of Teachers of English, 1967.

Herndon, James. *How To Survive in Your Native Land.* New York: Simon & Schuster, 1965.

———. *The Way It Spozed To Be.* New York: Simon & Schuster, 1965.

Holt, John. *What Do I Do Monday?* New York: Dell Publishing Co., 1970.

Jacobs, Leland B. *Using Literature with Young Children.* New York: Teachers College Press, 1965.

Jennings, Frank G. *This Is Reading.* New York: Teachers College Press, 1965.

Joseph, Stephen M., ed. *The Me Nobody Knows.* New York: Avon Books, 1969.

Kohl, Herbert. *36 Children.* New York: The New American Library, 1967.

McCracken, Robert A. *The Teaching of Reading: A Primer.* Klamath Falls, Ore.: Klamath Printing Co., 1970.

Moffett, James. *A Student Centered Language Arts Curriculum, Grades K-6.* Boston: Houghton Mifflin Co., 1968.

Painter, Helen W., ed. *Reaching Children and Young People Through Literature.* Newark, Del.: International Reading Association, 1971.

Petty, Walter and Brown, Mary E. *Slithery Snakes and Other Aids to Children's Writing.* New York: Appleton-Century-Crofts, 1967.

Possien, Wilma M. *They All Need to Talk: Oral Communication in the Language Arts Program.* New York: Appleton-Century-Crofts, 1969.

Rist, Ray C. "Student Social Class and Teacher Expectations: The Self-Fulfilling Prophecy in Ghetto Education," *Harvard Educational Review* 40 (3) August 1970.

Rogers, Carl. *Freedom to Learn.* Columbus, Ohio: Charles E. Merrill Publishing Co., 1969.

Rogers, Vincent R. *Teaching in the British Primary School.* London: The Macmillan Co., 1970.

Rosenthal, Robert and Jacobson, Lenore. *Pygmalion in the Classroom.* New York: Holt, Rinehart & Winston, 1968.

Sawicki, Florence et al. "Key Words to Reading: The Language Experience Approach Begins," *The Chandler Arizonian.* 1968

Silberman, Charles E. *Crisis in the Classroom.* New York: Random House, 1970.

Smith, James A. *Creative Teaching of Reading and Literature in the Elementary School.* Boston: Allyn & Bacon, 1967.

Vogel, Ray et al. *The Other City.* New York: David White Co., 1969.

Wolsch, Robert A. *Poetic Composition Through the Grades.* New York: Teachers College Press, 1970.